PERGAMON INSTITUTE OF ENGLISH (NEW YORK)

Language Teaching Methodology Series

Crosscultural Understanding

Other titles in this series include

ALTMAN, Howard B. and C. Vaughan James
Foreign Language Teaching: meeting individual needs

BRUMFIT, Christopher J.
Problems and Principles in English Teaching
English for International Communication

CARROLL, Brendan J.
Testing Communicative Performance: an interim study

ELLIS, R.
Classroom Second Language Development

FISIAK, Jacek (ed.)
Contrastive Linguistics and the Language Teacher

FREUDENSTEIN, BENEKE, PONISH (eds.)
Language Incorporated: teaching foreign languages in industry

FREUDENSTEIN, Reinhold
Teaching Foreign Languages to the Very Young

JOHNSON, Keith
Communicative Syllabus Design and Methodology

JUNG, Udo
Reading: a symposium

KACHRU, B.
The Alchemy of English

KRASHEN, Stephen
Second Language Acquisition and Second Language Learning
Principles and Practice in Second Language Acquisition

KRASHEN, Stephen and Tracy Terrell
The Natural Approach

LA FORGE, Paul G.
Counseling and Culture in Second Language Acquisition

LEONTIEV, Alexei
Psychology and the Language Learning Process

LOVEDAY, Leo
The Sociolinguistics of Learning and Using a Non-native Language

STREVENS, Peter
Teaching English as an International Language

TOSI, Arturo
Immigration and Bilingual Education

YALDEN, Janice
The Communicative Syllabus

See also SYSTEM *the international journal of Educational Technology and Language Learning Systems* (sample copy available on request).

Crosscultural Understanding

Processes and Approaches for Foreign Language,
English as a Second Language and Bilingual Educators

Gail L. Nemetz Robinson

Centre for Language and CrossCultural Skills,
San Francisco, California, U.S.A.

PERGAMON INSTITUTE OF ENGLISH

a member of the Pergamon Group

New York · Oxford · Toronto · Sydney · Frankfurt

U.S.A.	Pergamon Press Inc., Maxwell House, Fairview Park, Elmsford, New York 10523, U.S.A.
U.K.	Pergamon Press Ltd., Headington Hill Hall, Oxford OX3 0BW, England
CANADA	Pergamon Press Canada Ltd., Suite 104, 150 Consumers Road, Willowdale, Ontario M2J 1P9, Canada
AUSTRALIA	Pergamon Press (Aust.) Pty. Ltd., P.O. Box 544, Potts Point, N.S.W. 2011, Australia
FEDERAL REPUBLIC OF GERMANY	Pergamon Press GmbH, Hammerweg 6, D-6242 Kronberg Taunus, Federal Republic of Germany

First edition 1985

Library of Congress Cataloging in Publication Data

Robinson, Gail L. Nemetz
Crosscultural understanding.
(Language teaching methodology series)
Bibliography: p.
1. Intercultural education.   2. Socialization.   3. Intercultural
communication.   I. Title.   II. Series.
LC1099.R62   1985   371.97   85-558

British Library Cataloguing in Publication Data

Robinson, Gail L. Nemetz
Crosscultural understanding: processes and approaches for
foreign language, English as a second language and bilingual
educators.—
Language teaching methodology series
1. Language and languages—Study and teaching
2. Language and culture
I. Title   II. Series
418'.007   P53
ISBN 0-08-031059-1

Printed and bound in Great Britain by
William Clowes Limited, Beccles and London

To
Robert Politzer, Wilga Rivers, George Spindler and Freda Evans,
who influenced the development of these theories . . .

To
Naoko, Miki N., Kotomi, Miki T., Minae, Toshiko, Sachiko and Chisato,
my first Japanese daughters who brought these theories to life.

It's nonsense to think that learning about cultural diversity will bring about acceptance of it—the effect can be to increase bias. It's nonsense to think that understanding and acceptance is essentially a cognitive process (Coladarci, 1976).

Contents

CHAPTER 1

HOW CAN A PERSON FROM ONE CULTURE UNDERSTAND
SOMEONE FROM ANOTHER?   1

Personal, philosophical and educational concerns   1
Key principles   3
Selective, interdisciplinary approach   5

CHAPTER 2

WHAT IS CULTURE?   7

Introduction: definitions of culture   7

Teacher definitions   7
A behaviorist definition   8
A functionalist definition   8
Benefits and inadequacies of behaviorist and functionalist definitions   9
A cognitive definition   10
A symbolic definition   11

Summary   12

CHAPTER 3

WHAT ARE THE EFFECTS OF CULTURAL EXPERIENCE ON
PERCEPTION IN GENERAL?   14

Introduction   14
Culture, language and perception   14
How does cultural experience affect perception in general?   15

Content familiarity and perception   16
Organization of stimuli   17
  Anticipated organization and perception   17
  Preferred perceptual mode and experience: field dependence and field independence   18
  Formal schooling and its effects on field independence   20
  Potential biases   20
Input mode—ways of presenting information   22
Output mode—ways of responding   23

Summary   24
Examples   24

Conclusion   25

CHAPTER 4

HOW ARE CULTURE AND CULTURAL ROLES ACQUIRED?   26

Empirical perspective   26
Multi-modal transmission of culture   26

Emotion   27
Sound   28
Space   29
Time   30
Body movement and dance   30
Touch   31
Taste, foods and food sharing   31
Aesthetics and visual adornment   32
Cultural transmission and acquisition as an integral process   34

Philosophical perspective   44
When is the prime time to transmit and acquire cultural learnings?   46

Early childhood   46
Adolescence   47

Conclusion   48

CHAPTER 5

HOW DO CULTURAL LEARNINGS AFFECT THE PERCEPTION OF OTHER PEOPLE?

                                                                           49

Introduction   49
How does cultural experience influence social perception?   50

Cues   50
  Physical cues   50
  Behavioral cues   50

Schemas   52
  Person schemas   52
  Event schemas   52

Evaluation of others   53
  Central traits theory   53
  Projections of self   53
  Similarity   54
  First impressions   54

How do crosscultural misunderstandings occur? Actual dissimilarity of cues and events   55

Different cultural assumptions   55
Different ways of structuring information and arguments in a conversation 56
Different ways of speaking   58
Different ways of interacting: reciprocity of communication   59
Remedying misunderstandings due to actual dissimilarities   61

Cognitive biases   62

Tendency for consistency   62
  Status characteristics and expectation status theory   64
  "Halo" versus "forked-tail" effects   65
Cue salience   65
Faulty inferences and attribution errors   67
Salience and causality: "seeing is believing"   68
  Judging ourselves versus others   69
  Intervening in attribution errors through empathy and analogy   70

Summary   71

CHAPTER 6

HOW CAN WE FACILITATE POSITIVE IMPRESSIONS OF PEOPLE FROM OTHER CULTURES? THE ROLE OF ETHNOGRAPHY   **73**

What is ethnography?   73

Categorizing experience   73
Observer as participant   74
Non-laboratory setting   74

Obtaining cultural information for the content of instruction   75
Obtaining cultural information for use in methodology   75
Evaluating fulfillment of cultural goals   77

Do students in multicultural classrooms participate equally?   77
Do teachers and students perceive other students the same way?   78
Does language fluency mean a foreign-language student has a positive attitude toward members of the target culture?   78

Ethnography as a process which promotes understanding and positive interactions   81

Commitment of time   81
Depth of discussion and observations   81
Creative listening   82
Self-awareness: learning by contrast   82
The effects of being a "participant"   83

Conclusion   84

CHAPTER 7

HOW CAN WE MODIFY NEGATIVE PERCEPTIONS OF OTHER PEOPLE? A SOCIAL LEARNING THEORY APPROACH   **85**

Predictability: culture shock or culture cushion?   85

Learned helplessness: predictability with no control   86

Need for control or coping strategies   88

Types of copying strategies   88
Internal versus external control   89

Learning to cope through mastery: a social learning theory approach   89

Psychological matching   90
Similarity of the model   91
Variety of models and observation trials   91
Observation of positive consequences   92
Repeated exposure to graduated tasks   92
Learners "can do" judgments   92

Contrasts with other crosscultural sensitization approaches   94

Awareness through lecturing and reading   95
Self-confrontation: mini-dramas   95
Role play and cultural simulations   95

Conclusion   96

CHAPTER 8

BECOMING MULTICULTURAL   **98**

Multicultural man: myth or reality?   98
Developing cultural versatility   99

   Summary of processes   99
   Contrast with approaches in foreign language, second language and bilingual programs   100

Becoming multicultural: subtractive biculturalism, marginality or versatility?   100
Conclusion   101

APPENDIX: A CASE STUDY OF AN ETHNOGRAPHIC INTERVIEW   **102**

*How does it **feel** to be a student from India at Stanford?*   103

   Procedure: the key informant approach   104
   Why use one "key" informant?   104
   Finding my key informant and establishing rapport   104
   Cultural information which emerged   105
   Mira's background   105
   Asking the "grand tour" question   105
   American culture at Stanford and the culture of India: learning through contrast   106

Self-awareness and the making of a friendship   122

   Know others and know thyself   122
   Learning to listen: confessions of a talker   123
   Taking the time to go into depth   124

REFERENCES   **125**

INDEX   **131**

Chapter 1

How can a person from one culture understand someone from another?

MANY educational programs from elementary school through higher education are concerned with crosscultural understanding. Foreign language programs often aim to promote an understanding of other cultures; second language programs often aim to bridge the gap between the student's home culture and the second language and culture. Bilingual education programs are often concerned with integrating cultural diversity into the content and methodology of instruction so that equity of education may occur. This book is addressed to students and teachers who share these concerns.

This book focuses on the processes of understanding from an individual perspective: how can an individual from one culture understand someone from another culture? Perhaps the question might be more adequately phrased, "How can one person ever understand someone else, especially when he/she is from another culture?" The processes of crosscultural understanding assume understanding in general, from a psychological perspective. With these processes we integrate the influences of culture. In the context of this book, understanding does not mean just decoding someone else's verbal system or being aware of why someone is acting or feeling the way they do. Understanding refers to empathizing or feeling comfortable with another person. In other words, what experiences may theoretically help members of one culture positively relate to, respond to and interact with members of a different culture?

Personal, philosophical and educational concerns

Anthropology teaches us the importance of author or ethnographer background data in understanding any account of culture. My interest in developing crosscultural understanding is personally motivated by a concern for justice and kindness. "What will it take for one individual to treat another with kindness and justice?" In my home town environment I was shocked by the unkindness of some whites who shouted "nigger lips" to black pedestrians as they drove by in cars. It seemed unjust and bewildering when black passengers on a city bus paid the same fare as whites, yet were relegated to the back third of the bus. Then the Cubans came to town, bringing their different language and customs and were welcomed with "spics go home." In conversation, few people disagreed with the idea of respect and equality amidst diversity, but when it came to *doing* anything about it—sitting next to a black when the buses were integrated or speaking with a Cuban immigrant—actions (or non-actions) spoke louder than words. The look on one little black girl's face the day the city bus was integrated left an indelible memory. She was sitting by a window peering out. A six-foot-tall white football player from my high school threw his stack of

1

books beside her and remained standing. I asked him to remove his books if he wasn't going to sit down. Then I sat down. The little black schoolgirl beside me was trembling and a tear was in the corner of her eye. If that football player had just sat down, maybe he would have *felt* that the little black schoolgirl was not so different after all.

From that point on, my personal concern became the focus of my academic studies and professional career. The primary question became: "What created the divisions between people and what united them?" Thus began a journey into other cultures that lasted some twelve years. I lived with people who spoke different languages, who were racially and ethnically different, and who represented vastly different socio-economic classes.

Early on in the journey I became a teacher, committed to the idea of teaching languages for the purpose of helping students empathetically understand people who spoke the languages, as well as helping students of the diverse cultures represented in the classroom to understand each other better. Every time a new cultural barrier came down, the principle was incorporated into the next program. Some strange and wonderful things began to happen. The more culturally diverse the teaching strategies and my own interactional style, the more students from diverse backgrounds participated, the quicker their language acquisition, the greater their affinity to the target cultural group, and the more interaction between the class members, both inside and outside class. I remember the class in Spanish at Memphis State University. On the first day, the blacks sat on one side of the room, the whites on the other, with each group subdivided by sex. The official purpose of the language requirement at Memphis State was "to provide a culturally broadening experience." The task difficulty seemed clear! To my surprise, seating patterns gradually began to change. By the end of the class, the seating pattern was like a chequerboard. Black and white students tutored each other, exchanged notes and even rides to outside events. Not only did they appear to understand each other better, they surpassed the other classes in Spanish achievement based on the standardized departmental exam, including those particular black students who had been designated as "borderline cases" by the previous professor. "Crosscultural understanding" and "equity of educational opportunity" were just beginning to take on meaning. The focus of my teaching and research expanded to include how teaching and learning strategies might be diversified to promote increased understanding of students from one culture towards members of another.

I kept introspecting and analysing what happened each time there was a "breakthrough to comfort" and "ease of interaction" in a new social and cultural situation. "What made me feel equally uncomfortable upon entering the home of the world's eighth richest man and entering the impoverished two-room dwelling of a twelve-member aboriginal family? What happened in both places that made me leave as a friend? Why did teenage aboriginal girls avoid the family planning clinic and the formal white Australian nurse, yet listen excitedly about birth control after I told them I was on the pill? At what point did an eight-year-old Papua New Guinean child living in the village where I was staying finally approach me? What happened that made her slip her little hand into mine as we walked through the jungle? Why didn't these Papua New Guinean children appear to be able to conserve volume across different shaped pottery jugs until I made them put their hands in the water inside the jugs? How did I come to know the mother of my Japanese boyfriend on a farm in Japan without speaking Japanese? How did warmth and familiarity grow with each non-verbal visit? What was it that made Japanese students break through their defined domains of public and private meaning and share their most personal thoughts and feelings in the public situation of an English classroom? How did they function happily and successfully within a new relationship and interactional style between student and teacher? What kept Elizabeth, a fifty-year-old Polish immigrant, from being able to speak English and alienated from her Australian educated children when she was so desperate to learn? What accelerated her language proficiency and communicative competence?"

Key principles

Through observation, participation, introspection and analysis, some simple principles emerged:

1. On a one-to-one basis, the differences between people divided them, the commonalities brought them together.
2. Understanding, in the sense of smooth interaction, was probably least affected by awareness of how people were going to act, or the ability to anticipate culturally different events. Understanding happened through all the modes of perception.
3. Neither I nor learners were a cultural *tabula rasa*. Understanding of another culture did not seem to happen independently of the learner's or my own culture. The new cultural experiences were not "add-ons." They seemed to be interpreted through and integrated with the learner's previous experience.
4. Understanding—getting over the barriers to communication—did not happen suddenly; it took place gradually. Understanding took time.

While the point that "the differences between people divided them and the commonalities brought them together" seems obvious, most courses aiming to teach about other people, especially in foreign language and bilingual education programs, begin with the uniqueness of the culture studied—that which distinguishes the culture of study from other groups. (In Papua New Guinea I even caught myself taking pictures of the strange, exotic tribesmen wearing leaves and feathers, instead of the university students and boys in the villages wearing jeans who were equally visible.) Part of the problem is how we define culture. In Chapter 2 the different definitions of culture are discussed so that we may see how they influence cultural instruction. Another part of the problem is how we process information. Chapter 5 presents psychological explanations of how we tend to perceive and remember things that are unique, i.e., things that stand out, more than things which are common. The discussion explains theoretically why this happens and what curriculum writers, teachers and crosscultural trainers can do about it.

Second, understanding, e.g., that feeling of comfort and positive interaction, did not always increase with awareness of how the people were going to act. Non-observable, implicit aspects of culture, such as my own cultural interpretations and internal reactions to events were more critical to understanding or misunderstanding than knowledge I had obtained or failed to obtain about cultural values, customs or reasons for particular cultural behaviours. Understanding kept increasing as more of the senses were involved in the understanding of a single message. When I first went to Japan, I was aware that people ate raw fish; however, the idea was pretty nauseating. The first time I was invited into a Japanese home and saw the raw fish served to me, I wanted to heave, although I had correctly anticipated the event! I also knew that it was appropriate that I should politely eat it. (My instant response to that experience was to avoid a similar situation by politely offering my regrets at not being able to accept the next invitation!) My physiological mechanism did not understand, i.e., it was not congruent with the new cultural experience. The children in Papua New Guinea were able to understand the relationship between shape and volume when they *touched* the jugs and their contents. The Polish immigrant in Australia started speaking when structured linguistic exercises involved her and were congruent with her *emotionally*.

This book suggests that physiological, emotional, kinesthetic, tactile and other sensory modes of perception and responses influence understanding as much as cognitive modes which focus on knowledge about others. Theoretically, this idea is discussed from four perspectives:

(1) from an anthropological perspective involving the various definitions of culture (discussed in Chapter 2);
(2) from an anthropological perspective involving an original analysis of how culture is acquired, using case studies of a variety of western and non-western cultures (discussed in Chapter 4);
(3) from a psychological perspective involving cognition, perception and what people do when incongruent information is introduced (discussed in Chapters 3 and 5);
(4) from a socio-linguistic perspective involving what happens when incongruent elements are introduced into the speech situation (also discussed in Chapter 5). The idea of *understanding as perceptual congruence* within all the response modes is one of the key theoretical notions explored.

Third, the students were never a cultural *tabula rasa*, nor was I. I was never able to "step into the shoes of the other person." I had my own shoes on. I would forever have to contend with my own previous experiences, which included cultural experiences; however, my interpretations of these experiences were ever changing. The whole state of my cultural repertoire was constantly undergoing modification. Each new experience was somehow influenced by and interpreted through what I had already experienced and would in turn influence subsequent experiences to some extent. In the context of teaching, when instruction and expected student responses reflected the new cultural experience, combined with and interpreted through each student's own cultural experience, participation and language achievement increased. Chapter 3 presents a psychological analysis of selective perception, i.e., the influence of previous experience on subsequent perceptions. Previous experience is both individual and cultural. It is not argued that culture determines or fixes perception. Rather, it is illustrated that cultural experience, like all experience, does involve what we subsequently select to perceive, how it is interpreted and understood, e.g., is it congruent emotionally, intellectually? In developing crosscultural understanding in bilingual, second and foreign language programs, cultural experience of the learner is something to be applied to the whole learning environment, i.e., the teaching methodology, structuring of tasks, interactional styles, rewards and sanctions, criteria for acceptable responses and methods of evaluation as well as to the selection of content.

Selective perception and interpretation also involves the process of drawing inferences. Chapter 5 explains why people draw faulty inferences and make incorrect decisions about other people. The discussion is applied to activities for foreign language, bilingual and intercultural programs.

Fourth, understanding is a gradual process, especially when one is trying to understand something initially perceived as negative. The aforementioned breakthroughs to comfort and interaction were never sudden shifts. They were nothing akin to jumping in there, as in role play. In the example about the raw fish, downing the plate of fish all at once certainly was not the solution! In the classroom at Memphis State mentioned earlier, seating patterns did not change overnight. Distances between blacks and whites decreased little by little; seats were rearranged person by person, day by day, until gradually, the chequerboard appeared. The little girl who slipped her hand into mine in the jungle in Papua New Guinea did not do it all of a sudden. On our first encounter two weeks before, she had stood about a city block away. Gradually, each day, she moved a bit closer. The night before our walk she had sat in the back of a group who surrounded me as we sang together. During the walk she began trailing some twenty feet behind and kept decreasing her distance until an hour had passed and her hand was in mine. Chapter 7 explains the process of gradual change through the perspective of social learning theory. Social learning theory offers approaches to coping with differences or events perceived as negative which may add something over methods of role play, culture capsules and other instant cultural immersion techniques.

The systematic study of each of the above principles leads to the main idea of this book: understanding someone from another culture involves modifying one's own cultural repertoire, that is, developing cultural versatility.

Selective, interdisciplinary approach

In focusing on the teaching of culture, as with any subject, we often lose sight of the processes by which individuals learn. In teaching cultural understanding, we may fail to consider the processes by which learners understand. While the following pages do not offer an exhaustive or definitive account of cultural understanding, they do offer an interdisciplinary, though selective perspective to explore what crosscultural understanding and cultural versatility imply. This book is concerned with crosscultural understanding; however, explicit culture *per se* is not the issue. As mentioned in the beginning, the focus is on the processes of understanding and misunderstanding from the individual's perspective. Some of these processes may elude the learner's awareness. With a foundation of human understanding, we may better conceptualize the influences of culture on understanding and interaction.

In speaking to the American Ethnological Society, Spencer (1969) has suggested that inadequacies of previous approaches to cultural understanding are in part due to the lack of an interdisciplinary approach:

One of the consequences of deliberately sealing ourselves from contact with other disciplines concerned with symbolism, is that we remain unaware of the whole range of important conceptual and theoretical problems—not to mention conceptual systems, bodies of data, and methods of analysis—which could suggest important problems for us, problems which would then guide our ethnographic observations . . .

Understanding someone from another culture may be likened to a puzzle, whose picture cannot become clear until the individual pieces are first identified and then put together. By examining selected relevant theory from a variety of disciplines this book provides some key pieces to the puzzle. Many pieces to the puzzle have already been disclosed by others. Other pieces remain to be explored. Because the discussions are drawn from a variety of disciplines, the book may be viewed as a collection of theoretical essays on the topic of developing crosscultural understanding.

With the close of this chapter, I shift from my subjective tone to one more consistent with the theoretical discussions that follow.

Chapter 2

What is culture?

Introduction: definitions of culture

I know of no way to better ensure having nothing productive happen than for a language department to begin its approach to culture by a theoretical concern for defining the term (Seelye, 1978).

MANY educators emphasize the importance of "practicing culture" in the classroom rather than trying to define it. While this emphasis is well-placed, one's general concept about what culture is and how it is acquired will determine *what* is practiced in a classroom aimed at crosscultural understanding and *how* it is practiced.

Traditionally, culture and learning have been studied through separate disciplines. The methodological separation for the purpose of inquiry has contributed an artificial independence to these concepts. Anthropologists have traditionally been concerned with that which is collective, is *shared*; and educational psychologists have focused on the *individual* and the psychological processes through which individual learning takes place. Notions of culture as something which is shared and learning which is individual are generally known and accepted by most educators (although less generally translated into educational practices). What may be less understood is *what* is shared when we speak of culture and *how* it is shared—by what process? In other words, by what process do culture and learning combine so that culture is acquired? Let us begin with some familiar ideas about culture and see how they affect notions about what is shared in the name of culture and how culture is learned or acquired.

Teacher definitions

During the past three years I have begun my lectures and workshops on culture learning by asking participating educators two questions: "What does culture mean to you? What teaching activities reflect culture teaching/learning in your classes?" Participants have included over 350 foreign language, bilingual, English as a second language (ESL), and special educators.

When asked, "What does culture mean to you?" the most common responses formed the following categories:

ideas	behaviors	products
beliefs	language	literature
values	gestures	folklore
institutions	customs/habits	art
	foods	music
		artifacts

Often, though less frequently, participants also mentioned world view and way of life. However, they were usually unable to clarify what they meant.

In answering the second question, "What teaching activities reflect culture teaching/learning in your classes?", elementary and secondary school foreign language and bilingual teachers frequently mentioned "the study of holidays, celebrations, customs, and foods." ESL secondary school teachers and adult educators often mentioned the study of American institutions, such as the family, and daily life situations, such as getting a job. University foreign language teachers mentioned study of the literature and appreciation of fine arts, such as art, music and architecture, as well as political institutions. The above examples indicate how ideas about what culture is coincide with activities taught in the name of culture. Two basic distinctions can be made in the three above categories of responses.

(1) The categories of **behaviors** and **products** reflect a notion of *culture as observable phenomena*.
(2) The category of **ideas** reflects a notion of *culture as not observable*: something which is internal but which can also be explicitly described.

It is important to take a closer look at these distinctions, and others not included above, which are also relevant to what is acquired in the name of culture. For example, some aspects of culture are not only non-observable, but they also elude explicit description, such as aspects of cognitive interpretations and affective reactions. Other aspects of culture may elude identification because their essence is a dynamic, symbolic process of creating meaning.

An analysis of behaviorist, functionalist, cognitive and symbolic definitions of culture will help clarify these distinctions and their relevance to teaching/learning crosscultural understanding.[1]

A behaviorist definition

The current trend of second language educators is to view culture from behaviorist and/or functionalist perspectives. From the behaviorist point of view, culture consists of discrete behaviors or sets of behaviors, e.g., traditions, habits or customs, as in marriage or leisure. Culture is something which is shared and can be observed.

In the language classroom, this concept of culture often leads to study of discrete practices or institutions such as "a study of the family; how the French spend their leisure; buying foods in the market," etc. In the anthropological literature, behaviorists focus upon the patterns of behavior rather than the discrete practices.

The behavioral definition focuses upon observable patterns of behaviour within some social group. For this approach, the culture concept comes down to behavior associated with particular groups of people, that is, to "customs" or to "peoples" way of life (Spradley, 1972).

Much valuable data has been gathered through this approach. Descriptions of behavior have led to the idea of cultural themes related to particular societies. Behaviorists tend to focus on the behavior itself rather than on an understanding or explanation of why it is taking place, or under what circumstances it occurs.

A functionalist definition

The functionalist approach to culture is an attempt at making sense out of social behaviors. "What is the function of particular behaviors within the target society"? Again, culture is viewed as a social phenomenon. However, what is shared are reasons and rules for behaving. While the function or rules underlying the behavior cannot be directly observed, they are inferred from the behavior and may be explicitly described. Thus, the definition is dependent on observations of the behaviour. Frequently, these rules and functions are described by non-members of the culture, such as researchers or ethnographers.

Howard Lee Nostrand (1966) and Ned Seelye (1978) have advocated approaches to teaching culture in the foreign language classroom which are built on behaviorist and functionalist foundations. Nostrand's "emergent model" stresses an understanding of the rules of behavior. Seelye's book on *Teaching Culture* combines both the behaviorist and functionalist concepts of culture. A constant concern is to understand why people act the way they do. Seelye shows that cultural data which are often treated as discrete cultural tidbits, such as typical foods, may be integrated into a cultural pattern and related to the seven goals of instruction specified in his book. The goals reflect a "rational" approach to understanding culture. The assumption is that by understanding the reason behind a particular event, be it eating different foods, speaking in loud voices, or speaking in close proximity, learners will better understand and tolerate the person who is participating in the event.

Benefits and inadequacies of behaviorist and functionalist definitions

Behaviorist and functionalist approaches facilitate cultural description and awareness of why some people act the way they do. Students are helped to recognize and anticipate cultural behavior. They are also helped to become aware of the interaction between culture and behavior, both linguistic and non-linguistic. However, these approaches are insufficient in several ways. They assume that cultural behaviors and their functions can be objectively identified; that awareness and anticipation lead to greater coping; and that the important concerns of culture, i.e., what is shared, can be observed directly or inferred from observable behavior.

First, different perceptions and interpretations of behaviors by different observers, be they cultural anthropologists, bilingual teachers, language students or textbook writers, result in a methodological problem for designating exactly what constitutes cultural behavior. For example, one researcher might observe a Japanese smiling and infer the reason for smiling in that context is happiness. Another researcher might infer that the meaning in the same context is embarrassment. A third observer might not perceive the act of smiling at all, and perceive instead another behavior.

To solve this problem, some researchers ask members of the target society how they would act in a particular situation. For example, descriptions of some of the cultural behaviors specified by Seelye were based on how natives of the particular culture "said" they would act. Sixty-six percent agreement among natives regarding what they said they would do constituted a "cultural behavior." Once particular cultural behaviors are identified and associated with particular functions, care must also be taken to avoid stereotyping. Behaviors and functions change across time, across individuals, and within individuals, from situation to situation.

There may also be some discrepancy between what people say they would do and what they actually do. In fact, people are often unaware of the reasons for their behaviors. In this regard, behaviorist and functionalist approaches to culture ask students to understand culture in a way that often eludes members of the culture themselves.

Second (assuming that accurate identification of cultural behaviors is possible), anticipation of cultural behaviors which newcomers perceive as negative may actually increase anxiety rather than cushion culture shock, even if the newcomer understands the reason. (Chapter 7 explores the role of cultural anticipation in culture shock or culture cushion.)

Third, behaviorist and functionalist concepts of culture assume that what is shared in the name of culture may be directly observed or inferred from observations. Some anthropologists have suggested that too much emphasis on empiricism, i.e., on that which may be observed and verified, may hamper cultural understanding (Berreman, 1972). Members of a culture may also share part of an internal process, i.e., a way of perceiving, interpreting and creating meaning—which leads us to "cognitive" and "symbolic" definitions.

A cognitive definition

The cognitive definition shifts attention from the observable aspects of what is shared to what is shared "inside" the "cultural actor." What is shared is a means of organizing and interpreting the world, a means of creating order out of the inputs. The idea of culture as world view is related to this definition. According to cognitive approaches, culture is not a material phenomenon.

Culture does not consist of things, people, behavior or emotions. It is the forms of things that people have in mind, their models for perceiving, relating, and otherwise interpreting them (Goodenough, 1964a).

The cognitive approach emphasizes the mechanism of organizing inputs. That is, culture itself is a process through which experience is mapped out, categorized and interpreted. From this perspective, culture is like a computer program. The program differs from culture to culture. The program refers to cognitive maps. Unlike the somewhat fixed notion of world view suggested by Sapir and Whorf, the program is subject to modification (Sapir, 1973). Some anthropologists have distinguished behaviorist and cognitive approaches on the basis of cultural *behavior* in the former, and cultural *knowledge* in the latter; however, knowledge is defined in terms of the internal program or system of organizing.[2]

Teaching toward cultural understanding in cognitive anthropology courses generally involves trying to identify the way members of a particular culture, i.e., the cultural actors, categorize and interpret their own experience. Ethnography is a method of cultural description which tries to get at this inside point of view. (Chapter 6 is devoted to the use of ethnography in crosscultural understanding.)

By focusing on this inside perspective, cognitive approaches to culture add something to behaviorist and functionalist approaches. However, they are limited in two ways. First, exploration of the inside tends to be limited to knowledge conveyed through analytic, cognitive modes, whereas in fact, other sensory modes may also contribute to the type of understanding that occasions positive reactions to and interactions with people from different cultures.

Intercultural communication is fairly easy when it is "cognitive" or based on what we know, but experiential communication is nearly impossible because it is based on what we feel... (Porter and Samovar, 1976).

Chapter 4 suggests that other perceptual modes, such as physiological, kinesthetic, and emotional modes play an equally important role in cultural acquisition.

Second, cognitive theory is generally used to describe and explain the way other people process information and structure their world. However, cognitive theory has less often been applied to a pedagogy for learning culture on the part of non-members of the culture. Culture viewed as a shared *process* would imply an approach to teaching and learning culture which takes the learner's own program or internal cognitive map into consideration in processing the new, target cultural information. (Chapter 3 of this book explores this approach from the perspective of selective perception and information processing.)

A symbolic definition

Cultural understanding viewed as processing within the learner leads to a symbolic definition of culture. While cognitive anthropologists focus on the mechanism for processing, i.e., the cognitive map, symbolic anthropologists focus on the product of processing, i.e., the meanings derived.

Symbolic anthropologists view culture as a system of symbols and meanings. Symbolists ask, "How is meaning derived and through what symbols is meaning conceptualized and communicated?" Symbolic anthropology is concerned with the dynamic inter-relationship between meaning, experience and reality. Culture (which is the product of this inter-relationship) is a dynamic system—an ongoing, dialectic process, giving rise to symbols which may be viewed historically. Past experience influences meaning, which in turn affects future experience, which in turn affects subsequent meaning, and so on.

Meaning is the product, not only of the association of "raw" experience with an already-defined "code" of name, but of the integration of successive past and present (and future: we experience our expectations, too) experiences into a coherent whole, a life-world, which each individual creates, but also internalizes (the creations of others becoming one's own experiences) and projects onto his or her interactions with others (Dolgin *et al.* 1977).

According to this notion, meaning is not independent of experience, but rather is in dynamic interaction with it:

Symbolic structures and particular utterances stand in a genuinely dialectical relationship, in which both elements take on their actual character only as a product of their inter-relation.... It is in this dialectic— mediated at times by necessity, and always by an entire complex of social relations and historical processes—that meaning is continually taking shape.... For Marx, as for Hegel, the meaningfulness of social interaction is part and parcel of their creation—in thought and action (*Ibid.*).

This concept of culture as a creative, historical system of symbols and meaning has the potential to fill in the theoretical gaps left by behaviorist, functionalist and cognitive theories. This dynamic notion theoretically dwells on the *interdependence* between the derivation of *meaning within the learner and cultural experience*.

Applied to teaching culture in bilingual, second language and foreign language programs, this theory suggests that cultural understanding is an ongoing, dynamic process in which learners continually synthesize cultural inputs with their own past and present experience in order to create meaning. As such, cultural understanding involves a synthesis between the learner's home culture, the target cultural input and the learner as an individual. Chapter 3 discusses what is meant by "home culture" or "target culture," perceptually. (In other words, what types of experiences are synthesized?) Chapter 4 illustrates how culture is acquired through such subjective responses. Subjective, synthesized responses to target cultural inputs would suggest evidence of crosscultural understanding over objective responses, expressed in purely target cultural terms.

Like the potential implications of the cognitive theory, the implications of symbolic theory have not been applied to a pedagogy for developing cultural understanding within non-members of the culture. Many symbolic anthropologists do not view their task as one of developing meaning or developing understanding in our terms; rather, their principal task is to explain meaning, i.e., to find out how other people structure their meaning.

The essential vocation of interpretive anthroplogy is not to answer our deepest questions, but to make available to us answers that others, guarding other sheep in other valleys, have given, and thus to include them in the consultative record of what man has said (Geertz, 1973).

For our purposes, the *development* of meaning is critical. As stated in Chapter 1, we are concerned with learning to relate to individuals within these cultural systems.

While symbolic anthropologists have not yet widely applied the dialectic theory of meaning to their own methodology of studying and teaching culture, symbols and meaning, they have put forth an important theoretical framework.

Summary

Various definitions of culture reflect different theoretical concepts about what culture is, what should be studied in the quest for cultural understanding, and the methodology that is most appropriate. Bilingual and second language educators most frequently conceive of culture in the categories of **ideas, behaviors,** or **products** which are shared by members of a given group. Behaviorists treat culture as observable actions and/or events. Functionalists focus on the underlying structure or rules which govern and explain observable events. Awareness of cultural behaviors and underlying rules help people predict or at least anticipate how others are going to act and why. Classroom practices in second language and bilingual education tend to reflect behaviorist and functionalist perspectives. Less applied are **cognitive** and **symbolic concepts** of culture which are non-observable and internal to the cultural actor or learner. Cognitive anthropologists liken culture to a computer: culture is an internal mechanism for organizing and interpreting inputs. Symbolic definitions of culture focus neither on external events nor the internal mechanisms for organizing *per se*, but rather on the meaning which results from the dialectic process between the two.

Edward Hall (1959) has suggested that "culture is the sum total of a way of life of a people." If we accept this definition of culture, then "understanding people of other cultures" must encompass a variety of spheres. Each of the above concepts of culture addresses a particular aspect and, as such, none are mutually exclusive in their relevance. The danger of a particular definition of culture lies only in its exclusive treatment in classes aimed at developing cultural understanding.

By combining concepts of culture and learning, which heretofore have been treated fairly independently, approaches to developing crosscultural understanding in bilingual, second and foreign language instruction are likely to be more effective. Ultimately, learning to understand someone from another culture hinges on the internal development of new or synthesized meaning for each learner.

As people express their lives, so they are (Marx and Engels, 1946).

Notes

1 See A. L. Kroeber and C. Kluckhohn, *Culture: A Critical Review of Concepts and Definitions*, 1952, for a review of more detailed anthropological definitions of culture. The above discussion is intended to introduce the reader to major differences in concepts of culture and their relevance to teaching culture in bilingual, ESL and foreign language programs.
2 In the literature on intercultural communication, theorists have referred to this cognitive notion of culture as the "intrapersonal level" (Triandis, 1972). This cognitive level accounts for perception and misperception as distinguished from the interpersonal level, which accounts for communication and miscommunication. Misperception results from a signal "not of intended communicative value." Interpersonal communication refers to those messages which result from "conscious attempts at interaction."

Chapter 3

What are the effects of cultural experience on perception in general?

Anthropologists approach cognition from an environmental point of view—stressing institutionalized rules that are products of collective cognitive experience and that form part of the cultural environment in which individuals function. The psychologist on the other hand approaches cognition from the side of the individual organism that is acquiring cultural categories and using them in problem solving. One of the vexing conditions . . . is that the two points of view rarely meet (Spindler, G. D., 1980, p. 585).

Introduction

In order to understand more clearly the relationship between culture and learning, and the idea of culture as an internal mechanism for organizing and interpreting experience, this chapter focuses on the relationship between cultural experience and perception. First, *what* is the relationship between culture, language and perception? Second, *how* does cultural experience affect perception?[1] At the outset it is important to underscore that the similarities in perceptual processes among people of different cultures far outweigh the differences.

Culture, language and perception

The relationship among culture, language and perception is somewhat like the chicken-egg question: "Which comes first?" Sapir and Whorf believed that language determines perception rather than the reverse. From their perspective, members of a culture share a world view by virtue of the language which they use in communicating with each other. Particular languages channel perception or thought in particular ways. Perceived reality is "relative" to the language of the perceiver (Sapir, 1973; Whorf, 1956). (Understandably, this hypothesis has also been referred to as "linguistic relativity" and "linguistic determinism.") For example, a speaker of Japanese, by virtue of speaking Japanese, perceives the world differently than, say, a speaker of English. In support of this principle, Whorf cites the different uses of grammatical categories across cultures. Particular tense markers or the lack of them are considered to influence and define the concept of time. If a language has no grammatical marker to distinguish between, say, the past tense and the past progressive, then the speaker does not perceive or conceptualize these temporal distinctions. Different color terms across languages have been cited as evidence that members of different cultures perceive and divide the spectrum of colors differently. If certain languages do not have a color for, say, *brown*, then according to this hypothesis, speakers of that language do not perceive the color brown.

There are problems with this hypothesis. First, it is difficult to conclude from such linguistic evidence that users of different languages perceive the world differently.

14

Second, and perhaps more importantly, it is difficult to conclude that different language use is the "cause" of difference in perception. We are back to the chicken-egg dilemma. Later research in the perception of color actually shows that users of a particular language *can* distinguish between different hues even when their language does *not* have terms to label the distinction (Berlin and Kay, 1969; Brown and Lenneberg, 1954; Bruner *et al.*, 1966). Perhaps the more critical question for our purposes is not, "Does language determine perception?", but rather, "Why do languages differ?" For example, why do Eskimoes have twelve different words for snow? Why do color terms differ across languages?

More recent research shows that ecological conditions, level of technology and related socio-cultural institutions affect perception and subsequent language development rather than the reverse. For example a Papua New Guinean dialect which had not had exposure to the dye used in magenta did not have a word for *magenta*, nor may have distinguished the color itself readily on first sight; however, with the introduction of the dye into the local region, the color became easily perceived and a color term developed. Both color perception and language development appeared to be dependent upon the *sensory experience*. This has important implications for second language and bilingual education. If actual exposure to particular stimuli affects perception and language, then instruction to develop cultural understanding must provide students of another culture with target cultural stimuli or sensory experiences. Just telling students verbally about the target culture or having them read about it—indirect exposure through language alone—will not suffice to modify perception of non-perceived or differently perceived experiences.

Of course, study of the language, while not itself sufficient condition for developing cultural understanding, does provide some essential components. Whether or not language determines perception, we do know that it expresses perception and the categorization of experience. Here again, the chicken-egg dilemma. Once language itself becomes associated with perception, it becomes associated with particular meanings and values. Once these associations are made, language itself "filters" perception in some way. For example, paralinguistic differences across cultures show this effect. The same degree of volume may be perceived as anger in one culture and timidity in another. These cultural perceptions and values which are attached to communication systems and which cause misunderstandings will be the subject of Chapter 5. For the present, the purpose is to show how experience within a culture may affect perception directly; i.e., what members of a culture generally see, what they notice about it, how they categorize this experience, and how they respond to it.

How does cultural experience affect perception in general?

FOUR types of cultural experience appear to affect perception:

1. availability of particular **content** or stimuli which affects **familiarity** on the part of cultural members,
2. **organization** of the stimuli.
3. most available or culturally familiar **mode of stimulus input,**
4. most familiar **mode of response** elicited.

Content familiarity and perception

Familiarity with an object or event not only affects what we see in relation to the object, but also how we think about it, i.e., the mental operations we perform in relation to the event. Price-Williams conducted a classic study in this area. He used familiar plants and animals to investigate how African children of Tiv classified and reclassified objects rather than using idealized forms such as triangles and squares, which were not familiar.

First, a collection of toy animals was displayed in random fashion in front of the children. These were composed of pairs of animals; cocks, hens, snakes, cows and others the Tiv children would recognize. Then there was similarly displayed a collection of plants taken from the vicinity of the compound where I was living.... The children were asked individually to put into rows those animals or plants that belonged together. A record was then made of the reason for the basis of the grouping. After the first classification, the children were asked to put those that belonged together again, but in a different way. And to continue in as many different ways as they could (Price-Williams, 1980, pp. 589–590).

The findings showed that all Tiv children studied, aged 6–11, were able to group the objects that belonged together and regroup the same objects in three to six ways, depending on age. The objects selected for study could be classified on the basis of concrete attributes such as color and size and abstract attributes such as edibility, location, etc. Cultural experiences with the content not only affected the ability to classify and reclassify, but also the attributes the children used as a basis for grouping. For example, concrete attributes such as color and size were the basis for the initial grouping of animals; the more abstract attribute of edibility was the most common initial principle used in grouping plants (Cole and Scribner, 1974, p. 116).

The influence of content familiarity on perception is now widely taken into consideration in the development of "culture-fair" tests. The literature on bilingual education also recognizes the importance of providing culturally familiar content as the basis for developing skills such as literacy skills. Most often this principle has been applied to topics for stories in reading lessons or to direct cultural information within social studies units. However, a review of textbooks for the bilingual classroom reveals that the principle of providing culturally familiar content is less often applied to teaching skills in other subject areas, such as maths and science.

In foreign language textbooks, this principle of content familiarity for the learner is often reflected in the selection of topics used for the acquisition of basic language skills during the first two years of instruction; however, it is less applied to the acquisition of cultural and literary concepts in more advanced courses.

In English as a Second Language textbooks, such as those used in the United States, this principle is rarely applied at all, even within the first two years of instruction. On the contrary, textbook writers strive to provide "typically American" contexts to introduce language skills.

The above discussion suggests that the way students think about things, i.e., the mental operations they perform, is influenced by their own familiarity with the content. Therefore, culturally familiar content is an essential ingredient in introducing the learner to new concepts, linguistic and otherwise, in the second language, foreign language and bilingual classroom.

One might ask, "But how can we introduce *new* cultural concepts?" I myself have elsewhere cautioned language educators about using "hollow language"—language whose content does not pertain to the target culture—in courses aiming to promote cultural understanding (Robinson, 1981, p. 28). Obviously students need exposure to the target cultural context. The question is, "By what methodology?" The solution is neither a methodology based exclusively on the learner's home culture nor one based exclusively on the new cultural context, as is prevalent within most bilingual, foreign language and second language textbooks. According to the foregoing discussion, a more effective methodology would build a bridge between the old and the new by providing culturally familiar content as a point of departure for introducing culturally unfamiliar content at every level of instruction. Jumping right into the content and context which is foreign to the learner would be less effective.

Organization of stimuli

In Price-Williams's study of the Tiv, we saw that children conceptually organized material on the basis of the cultural relevance of the content. Similarly, what people select to perceive from an array of stimuli, which parts are perceived first, and how they are organized are also related to previous experiences. Members of a group tend to share a network of experiences, regardless whether the group is defined in terms of ethnicity, race, religion, sex, or socio-economic status. In this sense, each individual belongs to many different groups or "cultures." The critical point to be made here is that all people, regardless of the particular culture or cultures to which they belong, perceive and organize new experience based on their own experience (which is part shared or cultural, and part individual or idiosyncratic).

Anticipated organization and perception

There is a voluminous psychological literature which supports the idea that the perception and organization of new information is influenced by previous experience (cf. Freedman, Sears and Carlsmith, 1981; Lindsay and Norman, 1977; Taylor and Crocker, 1980; Zimbardo and Ruch, 1977).

We do not simply absorb all the information we can get . . .; rather, we take in information selectively, then classify, categorize, relate and organize it into a meaningful whole. . . . Preexisting cognitive structures organize the processing of new information (Freedman et al., 1981, p. 113).

Psychological research has shown that objects which are presented in a jumbled array, i.e., different from the anticipated arrangement, are initially not perceived. Even when pointed out, they take longer to perceive than objects which are placed in their anticipated position. For example, a large telephone, floating above a street scene in a slide, was not initially perceived by the majority of viewers under instant viewing conditions. Similarly, viewers did not notice that a large lamp in a livingroom scene was transparent.

When a briefly presented real-world scene was jumbled, the accuracy of identifying a single, cued object was less than that when the scene was coherent. Jumbling remained an effective variable even when the subject knew where to look and what to look for. Thus, an object's meaningful context may affect the course of perceptual recognition and not just peripheral scanning or memory (Biederman, 1972). (My italics).

Stimuli that are "incongruent" with our anticipations may not be initially perceived and may take longer to perceive. I asked graduate students in both Bilingual Education Programs and Teaching English as a Second Language (TESL) Certificate

Programs to apply this principle to difficulties learners may encounter in bilingual and second language classrooms. Bilingual education students suggested that learners who were accustomed to, say, nonverbal forms of praise, might not recognize when they were being praised verbally. TESL Certificate students suggested that second language learners might not even hear new sounds of the language that were different from their own sound system, even though the teacher modeled the new sound.

Another experiment known as the "Rat/Man" showed that new stimuli are organized and *interpreted* through previous experience. In this experiment, subjects were divided into two groups and alternatively exposed to two different sets of stimuli. One side viewed six stick figures of people. The other side viewed six stick figures of animals. Both sides saw the same seventh slide. The subjects who previously viewed figures of people almost unanimously perceived the last slide as a "man." The subjects who previously viewed figures of animals almost unanimously perceived the last slide as a "rat." These experiments as well as numerous others in cognitive psychology suggest that, *without intervention* people select and interpret stimuli based on their own previous experiences and expectations.

Biederman has pointed out that in the real world, things occur in some predictable relation to other things. As he stated in the last quote, "meaningful context" affects perception. However, what is considered a meaningful context or predictable within a context differs across cultures as well as across individuals.

What is the educational implication? Do not expect the learner to automatically perceive or interpret material that is presented as intended by the presenter. Students in a foreign language, second language or bilingual classroom, whose previous experience relates to a cultural context which differs from that represented in instruction, may not perceive the target stimuli as intended by the instructor or textbook writer. In a film, learners from different cultures may not be seeing what you expect them to see. Therefore, draw learner attention to those aspects or interpretations which are the intended goal of instruction, be it a particular sound within a word or a particular category of phenomena within a film, such as psychological themes, body language as in greetings, cultural issues, etc.

Preferred perceptual mode and experience: field dependence and field independence

Previous experience within a culture also affects preferred perceptual mode, originally referred to as "field independence" and "field dependence." The concepts field independence and field dependence originate in the research of Witkin *et al.* (1962).

In a *field dependent* mode of perception, the organization of the *field as a whole dominates perception* of its parts; an item within a field is experienced as fused with the organized ground. In a *field independent* mode of perception, the person is able to perceive *items as discrete* from the organized field (Ramirez and Castaneda, 1974, p. 65).

Experiences within a culture may contribute to the tendency towards field dependence—i.e., emphasis on the whole, or field independence—i.e., emphasis on the part. For example, one anthropologist hypothesized that hunting would require visual acuity related to field independence. At the same time, hunting skill would be stimulated by child-rearing practices which valued self-reliance and independence. In studying the Temne of Sierra Leone, New Guineans, Australian Aborigines and Eskimoes, this hypothesis was confirmed; members of hunting societies tended toward a field-independent mode of perception (Berry, 1966, 1971).

Perceptual measures of field dependence and field independence have also been correlated with ethnicity and sexual roles within particular cultural groups. In one study, Mexican-American boys, described as popular by their peers, tended to be field independent more frequently than Mexican-American girls (Iscoe and Garden, 1961). These differences may reflect learned cultural differences.

Experiences with certain tasks and differential reinforcement result in a facility for doing some tasks and an inability to perform adequately in others (Ramirez and Castaneda, 1974).

The concepts field independence and field dependence have now been widely applied to the literature on bilingual education, with particular reference to learning styles and teaching strategies. The term field dependence has been replaced with field "sensitivity" because of the negative connotations often associated with "dependence" in American society. Field independent and field sensitive teaching strategies are characterized as follows:

field sensitive strategies	field independent strategies
teacher	
1. models, behaviors and solutions (problem-solving strategies are modeled)	1. acts as resource person (solutions discovered by student)
2. expresses warmth	2. expresses formality
3. elicits synthesis; draws student attention to global characteristics, and generalizations	3. focuses on details; draws student attention to individual elements and varied combinations of elements
4. devises cooperative tasks and group projects	4. assigns individual projects
curriculum	
5. adapted to context of student experience (personalized)	5. focused on objective facts
6. use of student-developed materials (e.g., generative word method in reading)	6. use of standard graphs, charts, tables, etc.
rewards & sanctions	
7. social rewards	7. non-social rewards
8. non-competitive on individual basis	8. based on individual competition
9. varied & frequently non-verbal (e.g., gesture, touch)	9. mainly verbal (oral or written)

(Adapted and extended from *New Approaches to Bilingual, Bicultural Education*, pp. 72–73.)

Formal schooling and its effects on field independence

Western-type formal schooling may be viewed as a culture, with analogous effects on perception. Like culture as defined by ethnicity, schooling provides a network of interrelated experiences which school-goers tend to share more than non-school-goers. Western-type formal schooling emphasizes skills related to field-independence, such as analytical ability. Not surprisingly, schooling has been correlated both with field independence and analytical ability, as measured by the Wechsler intelligence scales. Schooling also affects how people classify objects. Without formal schooling, Kpelle children classified objects on the basis of color; children with schooling classified objects on the basis of both form and function. The incidence of reclassifying the same objects on the basis of a different criterion was much higher among the children with schooling, and reclassification among the school-goers increased with age (Cole and Scribner, 1974).

Potential biases

The attributes which are the bases of classification among school-goers versus non-school-goers are viewed on a continuum, with color being at the "low" end and function at the "high" end. Work of anthropologists also reflects the tendency to place on the high end that which is promoted by Western-type tasks, related to Western, technological, societal needs. For example, one anthropologist observed that primitive people had exceptional sensory powers, such as visual acuity. However, he concluded that these powers among non-western people were developed at the expense of higher mental faculties (Rivers, 1901). Higher mental faculties tend to be defined in terms of those skills and values which are taught within Western schooling. Clearly, Western schooling prizes independent thinking and critical, analytical abilities. Educational practices such as individual assignments, competitive awards, relative achievement, ranked scores, and even individual seating in individual rows, all transmit and support this value. Witkin himself places perceptual differences on a continuum, from global perception of the whole at the low end and discrete perception of the part at the high end. Since Western-type schooling prizes and encourages field independence, it is not surprising that field dependence/sensitivity and field independence are viewed on a developmental continuum with field dependence on the low end and field independence on the high end. As mentioned earlier, dependence itself implies a lower value in a society such as the United States, which is built upon the notion of independence and individual integrity.

One could argue that if too much emphasis is placed on analytical abilities, it is natural that other modes of perception should suffer. I am reminded of my visit to Mammoth Cave when I was five years old. The fossils of fish gave evidence that they had no eyes. The guide explained that the fish, through years in the darkness and subsequent disuse of eyes, eventually were born without them! As educators involved with linguistic and cultural diversity, evaluating the thinking processes of members of a particular culture on the basis of that which is functional to and valued by our own culture would be particularly unproductive. If the study of another culture is to lead the learner to another cultural perspective, it is critical that the new perspective be considered valuable and worthy of learning. Depending upon the culture of study, developing cultural understanding may imply that students are to become perceptually versatile; it may imply becoming acutely aware of color, or acting in accordance with intuition, or developing collective strategies for problem solving. In understanding a second language, if the grammar or phonology are not worthy of learning, it is doubtful that effective understanding will take place. In understanding a second culture, if that culture's method of organizing and transmitting information are not worthy of learning, it is doubtful that effective understanding will take place.

Currently, the organization of instruction in bilingual and second language programs tends to reflect the perceptual style that is characteristic of mainstream schooling; namely, field independence. Regardless of which target culture is studied, instruction is organized to promote individual achievement, ability to analyze individual components and to detach oneself from the object of study.

Even instruction in foreign language programs aimed at understanding other people whose preferred perceptual style may be field sensitive tends to be organized field independently. Similarly, the mental operations students are asked to perform, or how they are asked to think about the content presented, is rooted in the mainstream culture. It is doubtful that a student of Chinese could feel positively about modern Chinese culture without learning to participate in collective tasks and feel the satisfaction of a group product. In studying Japanese as a foreign language, an individual student report on the topic of Japanese Team Management might serve as a valuable point of departure to learning about Japanese culture; however, in isolation it would contribute little to understanding and working effectively with Japanese. It would also be difficult to provide bilingual instruction, say Spanish-English, which promoted understanding of both cultures, and equal educational opportunity for all learners, without tasks designed to promote global understanding of the whole as well as analyses of the discrete parts.

The goals of culturally democratic education are helping children to become bicognitive, to function comfortably and competently in both field-sensitive and field independent cognitive styles (Ramirez and Castaneda, 1974).

Labelling students on the basis of preferred or dominant perceptual style would also be unproductive. First, there are problems with the instruments used to measure field independence and field sensitivity as learning styles. Second, even if we could accurately identify cultural tendencies in preferred perceptual or learning style, it would not mean that all members of that culture perceive, organize or interpret information as culturally anticipated. While experiences within a particular culture, as defined by ethnicity, may contribute to the dominance of one style over the other, a given individual usually is a member of various groups (such as those defined by gender, socio-economic status, nationality), which also affects perception. For this reason, research which has tried to identify perceptual style by culture (as defined by ethnicity or nationality) has been inconclusive. For example, it has not been possible to conclude that Mexican-Americans are more field sensitive than Anglo-Americans because it is difficult to find a research population which compares and contrasts the variable of ethnicity while holding all other group memberships constant. In fact, research has shown more similarities in perceptual style among ethnically diverse members of the same socio-economic status (which in part is defined by education and occupation as well as income) than among members of the same ethnic and national group who vary in socio-economic status. The effects of schooling, discussed earlier, may partially account for this finding. Third, even an individual's preferred perceptual mode varies across tasks. While we cannot, nor would want to label individuals or cultural groups by perceptual style because of the tremendous individual differences, we do know that the socialization practices and experiences within particular cultures influence the perception, organization and interpretation of events.

Rather than labeling students, we can diversify the organization of our instruction so as to promote the development of dual perceptual styles and patterns of organization. In other words, educators can structure tasks to develop cultural versatility within students.

Input mode-ways of presenting information

In the previous sections we have seen that experience within a culture affects which content will be familiar, what people perceive, the mental operations they perform and how people organize and interpret what they perceive. Similarly, cultural experience affects the input mode which is most familiar and most effective for presenting information. For example, Deregowski and Serpell (1971) compared the classification behavior of Scottish and Zambian school children using photographs and real objects. The Scottish children were superior to the Zambian children when using photographs (i.e., they were able to classify and reclassify the photographs by color and function). However, when using real objects, there were no differences among the groups.

Another researcher also found that mode of presentation affected apparent perception among Bantu workers. He attempted to train non-literate Bantu workers in mines and factories through training films and safety posters. The training program was not successful because of the mode of presentation.

The visually presented material was being misinterpreted or not interpreted at all (Hudson, 1962).

This outcome was attributed to the lack of informal instruction in the home and lack of habitual exposure to pictures. While studying the conservation behavior of Papua New Guinean sixth grade children, I also observed the effect that mode of presentation has on behavior. A previous researcher had suggested that these particular children could not conserve volume across differently shaped beakers. The previous researcher made sure that the content of the beakers, as well as the beakers themselves, consisted of materials which were familiar to the children. However, he presented the task through *verbal* instructions: "If I pour the water into this jug, will it hold the same amount?" On repeating a similar experiment with the same verbal instructions, the children appeared not to be able to conserve. (To rule out a language problem, comprehension of the terms "same" and "different" were tested prior to the experiment.) However, by modifying only one aspect of presentation—by asking the children to put their hands into the liquid—they were able to conserve. While *touching* the liquid may appear extraneous to the task, it may not be extraneous to those accustomed to having material presented through handling objects related to particular tasks. I had continually noticed children watching the process of weaving, drying coffee, harvesting yams while in constant physical contact with a person and with the object. While my observation was only exploratory in nature, it does support the idea that different cultures use different modes more than others in presenting or "inputting" information.

Western-type schooling emphasizes the verbal mode of presentation, frequently accompanied by visual reinforcements such as two-dimensional black and white or color pictures, and less frequently by three-dimensional film or video. Informal education, particularly among non-school goers, frequently utilizes visual modeling of real objects and touch. The effectiveness of bilingual, second language and foreign language instruction may be increased by diversifying modes of presenting instructional material, in two ways. First, multiple modes of presentation, i.e., multi-modal inputs, provides greater equity of educational opportunity for culturally diverse learners, regardless of the concepts to be presented, such as language skills in the ESL class, math in the bilingual class, etc. Second, if the goal of foreign language study is "cultural understanding" and culture is in part a preferred mode of inputting material, then understanding another culture involves becoming perceptually familiar with target cultural modes of presenting and inputting material. Of course, this form of culture learning, like all forms of learning, proceeds from the known to the unknown (Piaget, 1970). In this instance the "known" would refer to the learner's own preferred method of inputting information and the "unknown" would refer to the target culture's preferred mode of presenting material. Teaching English and the American Culture in Papua New Guinea, according to the above example, might mean initially utilizing learners' familiar mode of touch, while gradually increasing the use of verbal modes, until learners were perceptually accustomed to purely verbal instructions. The reverse would be the case in teaching Americans about the dialect and culture of Papua New Guinea. American students would eventually become accustomed to learning through modeling and touch, without verbilization. Through such a process, learners in both cultures would become culturally versatile.

In contrast to the above, strategies in foreign language and bilingual classrooms tend to utilize one of two extremes in presenting material: either material is presented totally in terms of the target cultural mode, as in many bilingual education programs and English as a Second Language classes in the United States, or totally in terms of the learners' home culture, as in many foreign language programs around the world. As with the previous conclusion regarding effective selection of content, a more effective approach to presenting material builds a bridge between the two cultures, which joins previous cultural experience with the new, by using multi-modal inputs.

Output mode-ways of responding

Just as cultural experience affects which modes of presenting material will be familiar, cultural experience also affects the modes of responding that will be familiar.

In studying the depth perception of schoolboys and adult domestic workers in Zambia, one researcher found that the kind of response elicited from subjects influenced depth perception. Subjects responded two-dimensionally when asked to *tell* about the pictures. However, subjects demonstrated three-dimensional depth perception when asked to *construct* a model of the figures in the pictures.

It might well be that what someone is asked to do with a picture influences his attention to particular cues (Cole and Scribner, p. 71).

Just as the verbal mode is most frequently utilized in presenting material in schooling, the verbal mode is also most frequently utilized in responding to material. Within a foreign language classroom, this means that American students of Japanese might be asked to individually write a paper about *Ikebana*, the Japanese art of flower arrangement; while aesthetic appreciation, touch and movement characterize the Japanese experience, an analytic, verbal experience might characterize the foreign language approach. If culture is in part a way of responding, then second language, foreign language and bilingual learners will need to become versatile in their means of responding to target cultural information. Eliciting multi-modal responses to instruction will facilitate this process.

Summary

This chapter has focused on the effects of cultural experience on perception. Experience within a culture effects perception and learning in four ways:

1. **content:** the content that will be familiar to a learner, which in turn affects the mental operations learners perform about the content;
2. **organization:** what the learner will select to perceive, how the material will be interpreted, and how it will be organized, i.e., field independently, with individual elements perceived independently of the background, or field sensitively, with elements grouped together and perceived first as a whole.
3. **input modes:** the modes that are familiar to the learner in inputting or presenting information;
4. **response modes:** the modes that are familiar to the learner in responding to material;

Each of the above has important implications for structuring instruction in bilingual, second language and foreign language programs, in which the home culture of learners and the target culture of instruction differ.

It is possible to structure tasks within these programs which reflect culturally diverse content, organization, and modes of presentation, and which elicit culturally diverse modes of response. In this way a bridge is built from the learners' experience and familiar perceptual modes to the less familiar or unknown.

Examples

Graduate students of bilingual education at the University of Santa Clara were asked to structure such a task. One student's specific objective was to teach the syllable *ma*. She applied the above principles to a language lesson for first grade Spanish-English bilingual students as follows:

Content familiarity: Begin with a discussion about *madres* (mothers), and how mothers make good food. "What do you say when mama makes good food? m-m-m."

Organization: field independent and field sensitive
field sensitive: everyone works toward the common goal of making a mural of foods; the class makes *empanadas manzanas* (apple turnovers);
field indepedent: each student individually measures the ingredients for the *empanadas*.

Input mode: visual, auditory, olfactory, taste
Present lesson using story about a puppet named Memo. (Students hear story. See movement of puppet.) In the story, the puppet learns to make an *empanada de manzana*. The puppet cuts open the apple and learns it forms a star inside. Students cut an apple and see the star (touch, olfactory, visual). Then they eat the apple.

Multi-modal student responses:
Construct real models using clay;
write list of *m* words from an illustrated dictionary to discover new words;
use apple seeds to plant or make a collage;
discover which students have *m* sound in name;
sing a song using *m* sound.

The Stanford Status Equalization Project provides another example of structuring tasks to promote educational equity and respect for cultural diversity. The researchers suggest that status and subsequent achievement among members of different ethnic and racial groups is equalized more readily in a multi-ability classroom, which is akin to the concept of multi-modal inputs and responses.

A multi-ability classroom is one in which there are many dimensions of intellectual competence. No individual is likely to be rated highly on all these dimensions. Each individual is likely to be rated highly on at least one dimension. Thus there are no students who are generally expected to be incompetent at new tasks and no students who are generally expected to be superior regardless of the nature of the task. In a multi-ability classroom, one's skill in reading represents only one important competence: it is not an index of general expectations for success at all classroom tasks (Cohen, 1978).

In the multi-ability classroom diversity is applied to: (1) the organization of tasks (e.g., both cooperative/field sensitive and individual/field independent); (2) modes of presenting material (e.g., modeling and role play in addition to verbal explanation); and (3) acceptable modes of student response (e.g., intuition, visualization, and verbal reasoning.)
Appendix A contains examples, specifically applied to different levels of instruction in English as a Second language, Bilingual and Foreign Language programs.

Conclusion

In conclusion, cultural experiences do appear to affect perception and subsequent learning. Tasks structured for cultural diversity in each of these dimensions are valuable in three ways: (1) they provide equity of educational opportunity in bilingual classrooms; (2) they promote second language acquisition, since language learning, like all learning, proceeds from the known to the unknown; and (3) they promote the goal of cultural understanding in foreign language programs since one dimension of cultural understanding is the development of perceptual versatility.

I know how to begin the old matt pattern, but I do not know how to begin the new (Old Kpelle proverb, Cole and Scribner, 1974).

Note

1 In the psychological literature, "perception" specifically refers to the process of making physical distinctions, such as distinguishing color. "Cognition" refers to the process of making conceptual distinctions, such as classifying objects by their function. In this chapter, the terms "perception" and "cognition" will be used interchangeably.

Chapter 4

How are culture and cultural roles acquired?

FOR some time second language and bilingual educators have been concerned with the relationship between first and second language acquisition. The profession has learned a great deal about optimal second language learning conditions from analysing the process by which first languages are naturally acquired and the optimal ages for acquisition. Perhaps similar advances in the area of crosscultural learning or second culture acquisition can be made by analysing the process by which first cultures are naturally acquired. This process will be analysed from an empirical perspective and from a philosophical one. Then the prime time for cultural acquisition will be discussed.

Empirical perspective

An analysis of how culture is transmitted and acquired across cultures discloses three factors that might be expected:

1. culture is transmitted and acquired through all the perceptual modes, verbally, as well as non-verbally;
2. culture is transmitted within an integrated context, i.e., when signals through various senses or modes send the same message;
3. culture is acquired gradually, through repeated exposure to similar stimuli or events.

Multi-modal transmission of culture

In the last chapter we saw that cultural experience affects preferred perceptual modes and as such, multi-modal development, i.e., perceptual versatility was seen as one goal of culture learning. In this chapter, the use of multi-modes will be viewed as a means of transmitting and learning other aspects of culture, such as cultural roles, values and beliefs. Analyses of case studies in cultural anthropology disclose that multiple sensory modes are utilized in transmitting cultural learnings. This idea will be referred to as "multi-modal cultural transmission."

Cultural messages are transmitted through language, sound or rhythm itself, space, time, body movement, touch, taste, smell, sight, and even telepathy[1]. (That is, learning modes are analytical, emotional, kinesthetic/tactile, temporal, physiological, olfactory, and aesthetic/visual.) These learning modes are overlapping, and in many cases the distinctions are artificial. However, particular learning modes will be referred to as a useful method of discussing and illustrating how culture is transmitted and acquired. The more modes which are activated and integrated in the transmission of a single message, the stronger the learning appears to be. Also, certain modes appear to be intrinsic to particular learnings. For example, transmission of say, empathy, would require stimulation of emotion in the learner, while transmission of a particular motor behavior would require the learner to move. This idea of intrinsic mode may appear trivial, if not obvious, yet "how often have we talked about developing empathy toward speakers of another language without using any emotional material or stimulating emotional reaction to the subject matter?" (cf. Robinson, 1981).

Because of the lack of seriousness that is often attached to experiential education, especially in higher education, the following analyses will risk pointing out the obvious to underscore the academic soundness of using different sensory modes in transmitting cultural learnings in bilingual, second language and foreign language programs, *at all levels*. Let us now take a look at how different modes transmit cultural learnings across cultures.

Emotion

Emotion plays a critical role in cultural transmission. While it is essential to the development of emotional attitudes, it is also frequently stimulated in the transmission of other cultural learnings.

Catharsis is often used to transmit specific cultural learnings as well as to promote group affiliation among members of such diverse groups in the United States as the *Holy Ghost Sect*, the *Snake Handlers*, and human potential training groups such as *EST* and *Lifespring*. For example, during *Lifespring* basic training, participants engage in a variety of activities which lead to catharsis. In one exercise participants engage in guided fantasy: they are asked to picture two large doors which open to a junk yard; after going from heap to heap, participants stop at one barrel; they look through each item, searching for all the broken promises that parents and friends have made to them during their lifetime. The silence is suddenly broken by sobs and screams as recollections of painful memories emerge. In this exercise, visualization and emotion are utilized to transmit the learning: "It is bad to break a promise to others; people should learn to keep their word and their commitments." The use of catharsis in a variety of different activities during training appears to have the effect of promoting group affiliation among *Lifespring* participants. This affiliation may even be more strongly transmitted than specific learnings such as the one above. A variety of integrated, multi-modal activities transmit the connection, "emotion and *Lifespring*," while fewer activities during the short training period transmit specific messages, such as, "It's bad to break a promise."

Language fluency may be viewed as a complex set of cultural learnings. Development of language fluency is also related to affect. Lexically similar terms in two languages have different emotional meaning and intensity. For example, to a native speaker of English who speaks French as a second language, the phrase "I love you" will have a different emotional meaning and intensity than the phrase, "*Je t'aime*." The reverse would be true of a native French speaker who speaks English as a second language. Understanding a language from a native speaker's point of view would involve an emotional understanding, derived from emotional experiences associated with the linguistic code.

It may be hypothesized that a cognitive bilingualism may be acquired through study, memorization, and other essentially academic modes, but an affective component—a more complex and complete bilingualism—can only be acquired if both languages are used in real-life circumstances. Becoming bicultural may be a necessary step for both cognitive and affective bilingualism to occur (Herrell and Herrell, 1980, p. 90).

Elsewhere I have cited numerous studies which also support the relationship between emotion, identification with the target culture and language proficiency (cf. Robinson, 1981, pp. 30–33).

Burner and associates also found that while working with the social studies program, "Man, a Course of Study," stimulation of emotion was a useful means of decreasing prejudice of children towards the Eskimos.

By concentrating on the information-giving aspects of films on the Eskimos, prejudice increased, but by encouraging children to try to understand the feelings, they decreased the danger of prejudice (Bruner *et al.*, 1966).

In educational programs aimed at developing affiliation with the target culture and language fluency, stimulation of emotion will facilitate the goal; in educational programs aimed at developing empathy between people of different cultures, the stimulation of emotion not only facilitates the goal but, moreover, is intrinsic to the goal itself.

The use of emotion is a powerful learning device. "Institutions which may be invested with high emotional value . . . are not ones which can be lightly legislated out˙ of existence" (Kroeber and Kluckhohn, 1952). However, involving learners in instruction emotionally is considered somewhat suspect in formal, public schooling. There is a fear that indoctrination will take place. It could be said that certain educational goals, including the goals of understanding another language or culture, are meant to be realized only partially. Educators must decide for themselves to what extent these goals are to be fulfilled.

Sound

The transmission of culture verbally, through language, is a widely recognized field of study. Less studied is the role of sound itself in transmitting cultural learnings, apart from the verbal and paralinguistic messages that are often integrated with it.

The use of rhythm, such as in the beating of drums, and music, with and without words, is part of most group rituals. During initiation of the Arunta, an African tribe, sounds can be heard from the beating of logs on the ground. Community singing is an important part of the Church service of the Hutterites in North America, as with many groups. Chanting by the Cantor is an essential part of religious services among the Jews. The devotees of Krsna can be heard chanting *Hare Krsna* through the streets.

Among the Dinka of the Sudan, song plays a particularly important role. Preoccupation with oxen is a central theme of the Dinka economy; this preoccupation is expressed through "ox-songs" among the men, and songs of praise by the women.

Striped Ox, you will mix with the bulls and your father will mix with the learners of the Sudan. He is the expert of the South, his words are strong. No one can surpass him in the land of Kwol (Deng, 1972, p. 83).

The description of what goes on during the song illustrates the emotion surrounding the song as well as the integration of other modes:

While all sing and *clap* (the only musical accompaniment), a few in the circle *jump* to the *rhythm*. Simultaneously, some people, and particularly those whose relations are mentioned, make such *loud cries* that it is sometimes impossible to hear the words. These *piercing cries* are an *expression of joy although to the foreigner's ear they might sound like the cries of a woman in distress.* (*Ibid.*) (*My italics*).

According to Deng, the men's ox songs are cathartic songs because they play a cleansing role: "indeed, the Dinka call them *waak*, which means "washing" (*Ibid.*, p. 85).

In all of the above examples, sound is used in the transmission and acquisition of cultural learnings, and in the promotion of cultural affiliation. I have also found that the use of music, rhyme and rhythm facilitated acquisition of English by Japanese adults (Robinson, 1971). In the above examples, the use of sound, rhythm and self-expression is not a supplementary activity but rather an integral part of promoting positive affiliation among members of a culture, such as the Dinka, whose survival depends on cattle raising. In contrast, the use of song, rhythm and self-expression is often treated as a supplementary activity in second language and bilingual classes. These activities are usually disconnected from other concept learning. Books such as *Intensive English Through Songs* (Robinson, 1971), *Jazz Chants* (Graham, 1978), *Suggestology* (Lozanov, 1978), may be used to good advantage in second language and bilingual programs if they are integrated with the particular linguistic, cultural or subject matter concepts which are the focus of study.

Space

Culture is transmitted through the organization of space. Communal eating halls and communal housing arrangements transmit interdependence among the Hutterites. In contrast, individual family dwellings and individual kitchens transmit the value of individuality in mainstream America. The organization of space also transmits male and female roles. The following describes segregation by sex in an Appalachian Valley community:

Churches in the valley contain two ranks of pews, with an aisle between them . . . men congregate in the pews on one side, women in those on the other . . . But it is in the ordinary round of daily life, occupational, domestic and especially leisure, that men and women associate most noticeably with those of their own sex. . . . In a manner reminiscent of earlier pioneer days, small groups of men gather outside the county courthouse on Saturdays (Hicks, 1976, p. 47).

Women in this community are expected to have the household as their main sphere of interest and activity. In contrast, men's concerns and interests are outside the domestic realm. This role separation is transmitted and acquired, in part, through spatial separation.

Socialization practices are also learned through spacial organization. In the last chapter we saw that the American value of independence and individuality was transmitted through the rows of individual desks still prevalent in schooling, especially in higher education. Through seating patterns in which learners view the back of classmates' heads, learners are taught not to rely on communicating with others for problem solving. In a study of schooling in Harlem, children who were accustomed to sharing space in tight home quarters were admonished for preferring to sit closely together (Rosenfeld, 1971).

If we are interested in teaching our students to understand, say, the collective emphasis of people from another culture, changing seating patterns in the classroom may help students acquire this cultural understanding.

Time

The organization of time also transmits cultural learnings. For example, among the Krsna devotees and the Hutterites there is a very rigid structuring of time which transmits an emphasis on the group and lack of individual decision-making.

All phases of the day's activities are tightly scheduled ... the whole sequence of activities being imposed from above by a system of explicit formal rulings and a body of officials (Daner, 1974).

Similar patterns have been observed among the Hutterites:

The day is broken into small units of time that form a tight, although not rigid, schedule. This severe patterning means that the individual members of the colony have little free choice and few decisions to make with regard to time. Just as material objects are not owned by a Hutterite, he also has little concepts of private time (Hostetler and Huntington, 1967, p. 23).

Among the Hutterites and the devotees of Krsna, the organization of time is consistent with and serves to transmit cultural beliefs, collective *versus* individual orientation and authority structures. As educators we can also organize time to transmit particular cultural messages. It would be difficult for students to acquire, say, the concept of *mañana* in Mexico, in a rigidly-structured classroom which rushes from one exercise to another, without personal or social interaction. In teaching students to interact positively with people from different cultures, instructional time may be organized to help students acquire the intended message.

Body movement and dance

Body movement may serve to transmit cultural messages directly, as well as to reinforce messages transmitted along other modes. For example, among Black militants, a tight-fisted hand surging into the air transmits directly, "power to the people." It also promotes group affiliation. In many cultures, such as native American cultures, African cultures, Aboriginal cultures and Balinese cultures, cultural beliefs are portrayed directly through dance. Among the Dinka, dance transmits the dual importance of group harmony and individuality:

Dinka dance is essentially a group activity in which coordination and unity of action is of utmost importance. It is a truly impressive sight to see all the dancers jump up and down or stamp the ground at literally the same time. . . . But the significance of the individual is not overshadowed by this group spirit. The fact that there are points in the dancing when every individual chants his own exaltations shows the importance of song and dance to the ego of every dancer (Deng, 1972).

Dancing plays an important part of many celebrations which mark the acquisition of new cultural roles, such as the initiation of a boy into adulthood and wedding celebrations.

Frequently body movement is integrated with messages sent through other modes. In the study of school failure in Harlem, Rosenfeld noted that Black children had learned to learn while moving.

Children's constant movement in the classroom suggested to me that this was the result of living at close quarters at home, mingling with many others in a small apartment (Rosenfeld, 1971).

People across cultures acquire essential cultural learnings while moving. People greet each other through different movements, such as bowing, hand shaking, kissing on the cheek. Status relationships are transmitted through culturally defined eye movements, gestures and postures people take while interacting with each other. Movement, modeling and imitation frequently accompany initial concept learning in informal settings. In contrast, learners are usually required to remain motionless in their seats in formal schooling.

Asher's *Total Physical Response* method, in which second language learners rise to the task of listening comprehension, is a welcome addition to language learning. The key again is to integrate body movement with other modes in transmitting the same message.

Touch

It is difficult to separate touch from body movement; the distinction is used only for discussion. Touch is frequently involved in transmitting culture and promoting affiliation among group members. Chimpanzees in the wild gather together and physically embrace each other when an outside threat is perceived. For chimpanzees as well as humans, touch is a natural transmitter of comfort, consolation and feelings of security, unless intervened in by learnings which counter this natural tendency. Touch, like all the modes discussed, is used to transmit particular cultural messages.

Touch transmits messages directly or as an integral part of messages transmitted along other modes. For example, members of football teams in the United States often put their arms around each other while huddling together before each play. Verbal messages aimed at defeating the opponent are reinforced through the inter-locked arms, which promotes in-group camaraderie and solidarity.

In some cultures, touch may directly transmit reward or sanction, acceptance or rejection. In the study of schooling in Harlem, Black children were hit as a sanction. To the children who did not understand why they were being hit, the action transmitted rejection (Rosenfeld, 1971). In contrast, another study noted that Mexican-American teachers touched children as a reward. To Mexican-American students, who were accustomed to praise transmitted through touch, verbal praise did not transmit the same message (Erickson *et al.*, 1978). In American schooling, teachers are encouraged not to touch at all; the use of touch has traditionally been interpreted as a punishment. However, touch may serve a positive function in transmitting cultural learnings and promoting cultural affiliation. For example, in a bilingual teacher training program, the use of touch in praising student work could serve to strengthen an understanding of nonverbal forms of praise.

Taste, foods and food sharing

As with the other modes, taste and eating play an important role in cultural transmission.

Like the other modes, food sharing transmits cultural messages. Across cultures, holidays are marked by eating special foods. In the United States, turkey, ham and Christmas pudding are associated with Christmas; easter eggs and hot cross buns are associated with Easter. In Japan special cakes commemorate the New Year. Role change such as initiation ceremonies and wedding ceremonies are also marked by food sharing and special foods. Wedding celebrations in many cultures are marked by special wedding cakes. Roasted pig marks wedding celebrations in many cultures of Papua New Guinea.

In some cases particular foods transmit specific cultural messages. For example, during the Jewish Holiday of Passover, foods are eaten which symbolize the history of the event. The holiday is marked by two *sedars* which combine prayer, history, and specific foods. For example, it is recounted that the Pharoah of Egypt had decreed that the first-born male of Jewish households be slain. A lamb shank is placed on the ceremonial plate to symbolize the killing of the pascal lamb whose blood was spread on the archway of the doors of the Jews. The blood of the lamb was offered as a sacrifice by the Jews, and the angel of death "passed over" these homes. During the holiday, unleavened bread, *matzoh* is eaten which symbolizes the plight of the Jews who, in escaping from their pursuers, had no time for the bread to rise. Bitter herbs are eaten to symbolize the bitter times.

Within Catholicism, specific foods also transmit cultural messages. During the ceremony of communion, participants drink wine and eat wafers which symbolize the blood and body of Christ. Through eating, participants symbolically experience Christ's suffering and sanctity.

Cultural roles and status distinctions are also transmitted and reinforced in the context of food sharing: whom people eat with, what they eat, and how they eat, i.e., forms of etiquette.

In travels and research across five continents, I observed that sharing in food gathering, preparation, and eating promoted positive affiliation between members of the culture and myself. It may be that sharing in the satisfaction of basic needs promotes affiliation among those sharing the event. This may explain why touch and food sharing are such powerful transmitters of affiliation.

The use of taste, food, and food sharing need not be treated as a supplementary activity in bilingual, second language and foreign language programs. They may be an important vehicle for transmitting and learning specific cultural beliefs, and for promoting affiliation with members of the target culture.

Aesthetics and visual adornment

Aesthetics as expressed in the form of visual arts, decorations and adornments to one's body, also plays an important role in transmitting and acquiring culture. Cultural transmission through art has been the subject of numerous studies and therefore will not be treated here. Decoration and adornment provide visual stimulation through which cultural beliefs are transmitted and reinforced. For example, both the Dinka of the Sudan and the Hutterites of North America transmit cultural values in daily dress. For the Dinka, the carnal body is something to be nurtured. Sensuous beauty is highly valued:

It is impossible to exaggerate the importance the Dinka attach to physical attraction and wholesome-ness. . . . To be handsome or beautiful is a great asset, but "sensuous beauty" is much more than a matter of determinism at birth. A man is not an "ayur" because he is born ugly: He is an "ayur" because he neglects his appearance and makes himself unattractive (Deng, 1972, p. 15).

The cultural value of sensuous beauty is transmitted through ornamentation:

Dinka culture is full of ways of enhancing a natural beauty or making up for lack of it. The starting point is ornamentation; Among the objects of beautification for both men and women are beads and shells worn on the wrist, neck and the forehead, ivory bangles worn on the upper arm or the wrist, and the long metallic bracelet, coils wound on the arm by both men and women and on the legs by women . . . (*Ibid.*, p. 16).

Fashion, cosmetics and general advertising industries in the United States transmit a similar cultural importance on carnal beauty. For example, milk is advertised on billboards throughout the country, with a bathing beauty beside the slogan, "Milk does a body good."

In contrast, the carnal body is de-emphasized among the Hutterites of North America. It is considered temporal, if not evil. Physical attractiveness is not a primary consideration in relation to the sexes.

The primary factors are those which benefit the colony as whole, namely, whether the girl is a good housekeeper, likes children, is obedient to the colony, and whether the boy shows initiative in his assigned work and accepts the values of the colony (Hostetler and Huntington, 1967, p. 11).

As with the Dinka, the Hutterites transmit their cultural values through dress. Among the Hutterites the carnal body is de-emphasized through clothing which covers the body from head to toe. Typical attire includes headcoverings and long-sleeved shirts for men and women, as well as long skirts for women. Clothing is functional and uniform, which transmits communal orientation rather than individuality.

"By their fruits ye shall know them" is interpreted to mean that one's appearance reflects one's attitude or the strength of one's belief. . . . What shows classifies the woman, just as it classifies the building. Her dress indicates that she is: (1) an adult woman, (2) a Christian, (3) a Hutterite, and (4) that she knows her position relative to men. It also shows whether she is dressed for work, for evening church, or for Sunday (*Ibid.*, p. 21).

Adornment and modification to one's own body also plays a particularly important role in developing group affiliation. Distinctive modifications to the body and forms of dress distinguish group members from non-group members. In-group solidarity is thus reinforced visually. In some cultures, modification to one's body also reinforces identity within the group. For example, among the Dinka, the six front lower teeth are removed. Teeth extraction distinguishes the Dinka from other groups:

Three kinds of people met and some became confused: there were uncircumcised men, there were circumcised men, and men with unextracted teeth . . . Don't you see, our heads are marked and our teeth are removed? We are the ancient race of the Dinka (Deng, 1972, p. 66).

While less permanent than the above physical changes, dress and adornment also promote similar group affiliation among members of American high school sororities. The following description of socies or sorority girls in one particular study shows how dress transmits values and affiliations:

Normally, socie girls dress in very similar clothes, and they feel strongly that certain hair and make-up types and clothing preferences are the most tangible and reliable indicators of a hoody identity. . . . Dress identifies those who either reject socie values or who are insensitive to their standards (Schwartz and Merten, 1974, p. 167).

According to the sorority members, the "socies" were at the top of the status system; the "hood" or "greasers" were at the bottom. One sorority member describes a hood's vain attempt to look like a sorority girl:

What really looks silly is they'll wear the right clothes but wear a big bouffant hairdo. Loafers look funny with a dress. Just little things like purses or jewelry. They all have to blend together to get a perfect picture. You wear a dress with flats and stockings, not with loafers and knee socks (*Ibid.*, p. 168).

In all of the above examples, aesthetics and adornment serve two purposes: they serve to transmit cultural messages and affiliation to observers, and they serve to strengthen learning and affiliation on the part of the participant.

Adornment may also be useful in transmitting culture learning within bilingual, second language and foreign language programs. While it is neither necessary nor advisable for our students to imitate adornment practices of the people they are studying, some decrease or increase in adornment, which reflects the target cultural message, may serve to strengthen the cultural learning.

Cultural transmission and acquisition as an integrated process

The above sections have illustrated how each mode is used in cultural transmission and acquisition. In many examples, various modes were stimulated in transmitting and acquiring the same message. Single cultural learnings such as particular beliefs, as well as complex sets of learnings such as world view and cultural roles, are acquired within an integrated context. This allows repeated exposure through various modes. In the description below, notice how many different modes are simultaneously used within the swing ceremony among Krsna devotees:

Each person present takes a turn *pushing* the deities in a swing. Through this activity a person is *actively involved* in service to the deities which ideally should plant the seed of love for the deities in his heart. . . . An *elaborate*, cage-like, *pink-satin* swing decorated with pink satin ruffles, jewels, and *flowers* is brought into the temple. . . . While the devotees and guests are *chanting*, the pujari *carries* the deities up to the swing. At the front left corner stands another devotee, *waving incense* sticks throughout the entire ceremony. . . . As each person gets ready to push the swing, a female devotee *pours* a drop or two of *water into* the person's *hands* to purify them (*Ibid.*, p. 49) (*my italics*).

In the above ceremony, the message, "love and devotion to deities" is repeated and multi-modal. Participants are physically involved; sights are aesthetically pleasing; smells of flowers and incense fill the air as they chant and pray together while the sensation of cool water fills their hands. Within such a multi-modal, integrated context, it is not surprising that cultural transmission and learning are effective.

The following example of weaning practices among the Hopi underscores how the message, "interdependence" is also transmitted within such a multi-modal, integrated context:

The Hopi child, from the day of his birth, was being weaned from his biological mother. *Many arms* gave him comfort, many faces *smiled* at him, and from a very early age he was given *bits of food* which were *chewed* by various members of the family and placed in his mouth. So for a Hopi, the outside world in which he needed to find satisfaction was never far away. He was not put in a room by himself and told to go to sleep; *every room was crowded by sleepers* of all ages. . . . His weaning, then, was from the breast only, and as he was being weaned from the biological mother, he was at the same time in a situation which increased his *emotional* orientation toward the intimate in-group of the extended family—which was consistent with the interests of Hopi social structure (Eggan, 1974, p. 317). (*My italics*).

In the above example, interdependence is transmitted through an integrated set of multi-modal messages, including touch, taste and spatial arrangements. In this way interdependence becomes an unconscious emotional attitude as well as a conscious value, transmitted through the total environment.

Similarly, the Hutterite world view is transmitted through all the learning modes. Each mode transmits the same message: "Good is achieved in life only by surrender of the individual will to the will of God as manifest in the believing *community* where all material goods and spiritual gifts are *shared in common*" (Hostetler and Huntington, p. 16) (*my italics*).

As we saw in earlier examples, time patterns are communally and tightly structured; space is shared. Hutterites engage in frequent group song, frequent group prayer, and frequent group meals. Dress is uniform and de-emphasizes the carnal body. Again, within such a multi-modal, integrated context, providing repeated exposure to the same concept, it is not surprising that cultural transmission and subsequent learning is effective.

Hutterite child rearing and socialization practices are phenomenally successful in preparing the individual for communal life. The individual is taught to be obedient, submissive, and dependent upon human support and contact. Socialization is *consistent* and *continuous* in all age groups (Hostetler and Huntington, p. 111) (*my italics*).

As mentioned earlier, language may be viewed as a complex set of cultural learnings. Compare the above examples of message transmission with typical language exercises in second language and foreign language programs. For the goal of learning the plural form of nouns and verbs, students are sometimes asked to rewrite disconnected sentences:

Model: *El chico es guapo.* (The boy is handsome.)
Answer: *Los chicos son guapos.* (The boys are handsome.)
1. *La montaña es alta.* (The mountain is high.)
2. *El amigo es simpático.* (The friend is kind.)
3. *La comida es buena.* (The food is good.)

(*Spanish Grammar*, 1972)

Similarly, for the goal of question formation, students are often asked to form questions from a disconnected array of sentences such as:

1. The students are busy.   **(Response)**: Are they busy?
2. The dog is hungry.

(*Dasher*, 1982)

Students are asked to learn the negative by changing disconnected sentences in the affirmative to the negative.

Model: *Me gusta jugar al tenis.* (I like to play tennis.)
Answer: *No me gusta jugar al tenis.* (I do not like to play tennis.)
1. *Yolanda es alta.* (Yolanda is tall.)
2. *Uds. son jóvenes.* (You are young.)

(*Chocolate y Churros*)

Pronunciation exercises are also often composed of disconnected sentences:

Contrast [ae] [u] **(Paired sentences)**
I found a ____ under the table. (bag, bug)
Hand me that ____ (cup, cap)
I caught the ____ in the boat. (bus, bass)
There is a small ____ in the boat. (paddle, puddle)

(*Drills and Exercises in English Pronunciation*, 1971)

The above exercises do not reflect prevalent theories of language acquisition and communicative competence, which are marked by authenticity of speech and meaning in terms of the speaker's intention to communicate. It is self-evident that these examples lack authenticity of speech from a native speaker's point of view and would probably fail to reflect any speaker's intention because people simply do not communicate in disconnected sentences or words. We read things on a particular topic. We hear speech within a particular context, and we write things pertaining to a particular context. Yet such disconnected items which lack any authentic meaning are common to second and foreign language exercises in textbooks, as well as in recently developed computer software.

While visiting a Spanish-English bilingual classroom in 1982, I found students copying the following sentences, as part of their English reading class:

I have a car.
Tell me why did you go?
I live in a yellow house.
I took a ball out.
How can you say that?

Would you be surprised to find attention and discipline problems in that class? Compare the above exercise with the following:

A box is black.
That horse can run fast.
A peach is white and red.
A cow gives milk.

The above exercise was given to me recently by my aunt, who was reminiscing about her childhood schooldays. She was proud that she had scored 100 on copying the items in *1914*! It is said that there is always a time lag for theory to be interpreted into practice, but from 1914 to 1984?

All of these examples are contrasted with the former examples of natural cultural acquisition, not only in lack of an integrated context, but also in the lack of multi-modal transmission. Acquisition rests on verbal, analytical modes alone.

Many texts include "cultural notes" or discussions set apart from the language exercises. It is not uncommon to find a collection of discrete, unrelated topics about the target culture as in a *potpourri* or smattering of experiences, without any intentional interrelationship among them. First and second year language programs typically present some discrete item linguistic exercises, in which the items within exercises as well as across exercises switch from topic to topic: some literature, some current affairs, some films and perhaps some recipes (Robinson, 1981). Repeated exposure to ideas within an integrated context less frequently occurs.

"Discrete point" instruction is not only unrepresentative of the process by which culture is naturally acquired, according to the anthroplogical studies reviewed; it is equally unrepresentative of all individual learning and language learning in particular, from the point of view of human memory. Research from cognitive psychology and psycholinguistics provides convincing evidence that items presented within an integrated context are recalled from memory more frequently than discrete items presented in disconnected arrays. For example, Clark and Clark (1977) presented one group of subjects with lists of ten totally unrelated nouns which they were told to memorize. The experimental group was instructed to learn the words in each list by creating a sentence or small story which contained all the words in one context. The following is an example of one subject's response. (The capitalized words indicate the key words to be learned.)

A VEGETABLE can be a useful INSTRUMENT for a COLLEGE student. A carrot can be a NAIL for your FENCE or BASIN. A MERCHANT of the QUEEN would SCALE that fence and feed the carrot to a GOAT (Clark and Clark, 1977).

On a delayed recall test, "Subjects who had made up stories were able to recall correctly 94% of the words from all the lists, as compared with only 14% for the control subjects" (*Ibid.*). In this study we have the opportunity of isolating the variable, "integrated context" from other factors, such as authenticity of speech. It is doubtful that the above study would fit into the parameters of communicative competence in terms of authenticity of speaker intention. However, the integrated context still clearly improved memory of semantically discrete items.

The previous examples of language exercises from textbooks and computer software lack both authenticity and integrated context. As such, they are inadequate in terms of language acquisition *per se*; and they are hollow in terms of cultural acquisition because they are devoid of any cultural concepts pertaining to either the home culture or the target culture. (One could, of course, say they do indeed reflect the culture of schooling!)

Is it any wonder people believe that learning a foreign language in school, without going to the country, is so difficult? Is it any wonder people believe that it is necessary to go to a particular country to really understand the people?

Repeated exposure through multi-modes facilitates and strengthens acquisition of the language itself as well as particular cultural concepts. Let us look at some applications to language instruction. In one class, English as a Foreign Language students at Stanford University went on a walking vocabulary tour of the campus. As we walked around together, students identified things they did not know. Each time they did not know the English word for something they saw, they were instructed to ask the questions, "What's this? What's that? What are these? What are those?" At this stage, the focus was only on correct pronunciation of /ts/ and /th/, which presents difficulties for Japanese speakers. Then the students wrote down the unknown words on an index card. Unknown vocabulary items included: *arch, sprinklers, ivy, crickets, lamp* and *palm trees*. For homework, students were instructed to make up a short story using their imagination and including as many new vocabulary words as possible from the walk. Here is an example of one student response:

Looking for Truth

A boy is walking through the woods one day. As he walks he hears what he believes to be *crickets*. Soon he comes upon an *arch*. The arch makes him curious, and he thinks the crickets are on the other side. After he walks through the arch, the sounds of the crickets are very loud. Here there is only *ivy* and no trees. It is very dark, and as he walks through the ivy, he cannot see the crickets. When he is in the middle of the ivy, a *lamp* lights the field.

He is very surprised to see all the ivy taking a shower under the *sprinklers*. Because of this sight, he falls to his knees and cries. The ivy watches the boy without doing anything, but it has a heart (Konomi Oishi).

In a Bilingual Teacher Training Programme at the University of Santa Clara, students were instructed to create one integrated unit of work for Spanish Language

Arts in which various exercises focused on different reading skills, including; decoding, vocabulary development, sentence writing, story comprehension/analysis. One student was interested in teaching the sound /t/, through a syllabic approach (ta/ te/ti/to/tu), to second and third grade students. She wrote her own story in Spanish about a timid toad, named Tito, who lived in the town of Tabachin. Although Tito was timid, he was helpful to his neighbours. In the course of the story, the toad was chased through a tunnel by a terrible tiger, but he was helped by the wise men of the village.

Lesson one—decoding: letter recognition and production through modeling, copying, and matching: exercises

1. Teacher *reads* the first paragraph of the story.
2. Teacher *shows* students a photograph of a toad.
3. Students *draw* their own toad and write the word, "toad," beneath it, *underlining* the /t/.
4. Teacher writes the first paragraph on the board and the students *copy* it.
5. Students *circle* each /t/ in the paragraph. Then the students underline each syllable /ta/ that they find.
6. Students write a list of all words containing the syllable /ta/. The same method is used to recognize the syllables /te/, /ti/, /to/, /tu/.
7. Students interview a student who has a syllable with /t/ in his/her name. Interviewer must use at least three words beginning with /t/ from the story.
8. Students select one word from the paragraph, e.g. *timido* (timid). Students divide words into syllables, and make all the vowel combinations possible with each consonant:

    ta te ti to tu
    ma me mi mo mu
    da de di do du

9. Students make as many words as possible by combining the above syllables.

Lesson two—vocabulary development: exercises

1. Teacher reads entire story, showing illustrations.
2. Class is divided into three teams. Each team plays the toad, tiger or wise men going through the tunnel. Teacher writes the name of each team on the board, and students stand in front of name for their team. There is one tunnel for each team. The team to get through the tunnel first wins. The objective is to extend the vocabulary by developing a list of characteristics for each story character represented by each team. Before going through the tunnel, each student must think of a characteristic of the person or animals/he is playing.
3. Teacher writes the characteristics of each character on the board, beneath the team name. Students copy the lists and underline or circle various syllables as instructed by the teacher, e.g., circle all the syllables with /ta/; underline all the syllables with /mi/.
4. Teacher develops a grid containing the words generated by the students. Students find and circle the following words, given below in Spanish:

tunel	tigre	son
topo	*triste*	*tímido*
pueblo	*cobarde*	*Tabachin*
tiene	*tapar*	*vergüenza*
todo	*comida*	*casa*

t	u	n	e	l	o	x	f	n
o	i	v	q	r	d	j	t	e
p	u	e	b	l	o	v	i	t
o	s	r	n	p	t	l	m	a
t	i	g	r	e	a	b	i	b
r	w	u	u	p	p	c	d	a
i	k	e	d	r	a	b	o	c
s	o	n	y	s	r	d	o	h
t	l	z	a	u	s	t	r	i
e	n	a	d	i	m	o	c	n

Lesson three—sentence writing: exercises

1. Students put story sentences into correct order by cutting out and rearranging the words.
   Example: a was timid Tito toad
   Response: Tito was a timid toad.
2. Teacher puts correct order on the board. Students check their work, match and reorder if necessary, and copy correctly.
3. Class is divided into four groups. Each group is given line drawings of the story illustrations without captions. Each group writes sentences to describe what is going on in the picture, and colors the illustrations.
4. Each group shows an illustration and reads caption, placing the illustration and caption on the bulletin on chalk board. Class puts the illustrations and captions in order until the story is completed.
5. Each student selects a word from the story and develops his/her own story, or teacher begins a sentence with words from the story and students complete, e.g., "One time I felt timid because . . ."

Lesson 4—story comprehension: exercises

1. Descriptive phase: teacher reads story; asks factual questions to test comprehension; e.g., "What was Tito?, What was he like?, Where did he live?" etc.
2. Interpretive phase: teacher asks students to interpret feelings of characters in particular situations throughout the story; e.g., "How do you think the wise men felt when they were trapped in the tunnel? Have you ever been trapped anywhere? How would you feel?"
3. Critical phase: teacher asks students to offer different solutions and points of view to the story, e.g., "Why do you think the wise men were able to finally trap the tiger? What do you think would have happened if the toad did not want to help his neighbours?"
4. Creative phase: one of the previous captions developed by students is given to each student without any illustration; class learns to make slides; each student makes a slide to give his/her own interpretation of the caption. (Jennifer Wood)

While each of the above lessons changed focus in terms of the particular linguistic objective, the topic remained the same—to provide an integrated context and subsequent reinforcement of learning. In addition, a variety of modes were used in transmitting and acquiring instructional concepts.

Many language and cultural immersion programs fail to take advantage of the natural reinforcement provided by integrating topics of study. For example, most university ESL summer immersion programs offer formal language classes, guest lectures, and sightseeing activities. However, these activities are commonly not related to each other. During the span of one or two months, summer students are bombarded with a barrage of different concepts, vocabulary and experiences. I remember one occasion in which foreign university students in such a summer immersion program attended a lecture on "The Melting Pot Theory." In language class prior to the lecture, students were instructed to listen attentively and write the lecturer a letter afterwards, commenting on the lecture. The following is an example of one student's response:

Dear Professor Jones,

Today you gave us a very nice lecture. I was glad to hear it. I went to hear the lecture with keen interest, but I could not understand what you said, because I was unable to hear and understand the English.

I was very sorry. If I could hear your lecture in Japanese, I could get more deeply involved with it. When I return to Japan I want to find a book about "the melting pot" to read.

Truly yours,
Konomi Oishi

To counter such a problem, an experimental program was designed at the Center for Language and Crosscultural Skills, San Francisco, in which cultural concepts and linguistic goals were mutually reinforcing, and were reinforced through every program activity. The principles of integrated context and multi-modal acquisition were used throughout a one-month intensive language and cultural seminar. The participants were Japanese university women, aged 19–21. The seminar was organized around four cultural themes:

1. America, the Great Melting Pot: how ethnic composition influences diversity in all dimensions.
2. American Government: concepts of freedom, responsibility, and citizens' rights,
3. American Technology: scientific achievements and the effects of technology on society and communication,
4. American Sports and Play: how Americans relate to each other in play, from the notion of competition to the new movement towards 'New Games' and cooperative play.

Each week a new theme was introduced. A bridge was always built between the themes; that is, themes were treated comprehensively. All language exercises, academic lectures, on-site workshops and sightseeing activities were integrated with each theme, both within individual exercises and across all exercises and activities. Students responded to each activity intellectually, emotionally, physically and artistically. For example, during the week in which the theme of technology was introduced, students were introduced to pertinent vocabulary and concepts in the language classes. In the first language class of the week, students developed a vocabulary list of all the uses of technology in their American residence. Then they compared these with technological appliances in their Japanese homes. In this way a bridge was built from their known experience with technology to the new concepts they were about to explore. Student discussion about the relationship between technology and society concluded with the idea that Japan is a leader in the production of technology, but America is a leader in its implementation for everyday home use. Students visited the California wine industry, the Exploratorium, the Planetarium, and the Computer Center at the Lawrence Hall of Science. Students had to communicate their feelings about technology verbally as well as visually in their individual scrapbooks and their group art projects. Students also visited the Stanford Linear Accelerator and thought about pure scientific research, nuclear energy, and the relationship between this and our previous theme of government and technology. In language class they studied articles about the pros and cons of nuclear energy development. They focused on pronunciation, vocabulary, and content, respectively. One article dealt with the role of individual responsibility in technological development. Then they heard a lecture by the author of one article, Bill Perry, former Chief of Public Relations of America's largest weapons building laboratory, the Lawrence Livermore Laboratory. He spoke about very abstract concepts such as the relationship between government and technology and empowerment of the individual. To my astonishment, the girls continually interrupted the speaker, debating issues, asking questions, asking for clarification. In Japanese conversational etiquette, it is improper to interrupt the speaker or to question a person of higher status. It is also improper to call attention to oneself and one's own ideas in such a public situation. However, in previous language classes the students had overcome their own cultural inhibition of interrupting the speaker and standing out from the group through numerous interrupting games. They had also been introduced to the concepts that were presented; they had developed the vocabulary, and they had developed listening comprehension. During the lecture, some cried at the thought of nuclear holocaust and stories of Hiroshima. Others argued the economic value of war and the positive benefits of nuclear development. These female, literature majors, at first uninterested in technology (by self-admission), had now used technology in the residence. They had walked through experiments and touched them, initially not understanding one word from their guides. Now they found themselves in deep thought and debate with one of America's leaders in nuclear disarmament, and they could understand!

The next language class focused on the relationship between science and creativity: "much of what is now scientific truth begins as the creative imagination." Within this context, students were engaged in the following activities:

1. Students read an excerpt from a science fiction novel by Kurt Vonnegut, Jr., "The Manned Missiles," in *Welcome to the Monkey House*. First students read the excerpt for understanding content. They answered factual questions to check comprehension.
   Then students read particular passages, focusing on specific pronunciation problems.
2. Each student chose a topic for a science fiction story. The topic had to reflect

both technology and student imagination. Students wrote down their own topics.

3. Students and teacher moved to the art room. Each student read her suggested topic to the class. The class voted on one topic to compose a group story about. They chose the topic that they were travelling through the fourth dimension, fell through a black hole in the universe and arrived at a planet just like Earth, but where everything was in reverse! They even spoke English, but in reverse. To form the group story, each person stopped in the middle of a sentence, usually at a conjunction. The group story was written on the art room wall as it was composed. The story below is what resulted: (Each . . . indicates a different student's contribution.)

> When I made a trip to an unexplored region of India, suddenly . . . I dropped into the black hole. In the hole I saw a light far away, and . . . the light pulled me, so I had to go far away against my will; therefore . . . I entered a strange world. I saw some spacemen there and they spoke to me, but I couldn't understand what they said, because . . . their language was very similar to English, but in reverse. They were very familiar to me and . . . strangely I was able to understand their feelings, but . . . when they were happy, they cried and when they were sad they laughed. That didn't surprise me; however . . . when they cried their tears went upward and the color of the tears was rose and sweet smelling . . . So I was welcomed by the flood of tears. The women who were there wore trousers and the men wore skirts, and the women were stronger than the men. The men were fighting for equality. There were many meetings of men's rights and . . . I, as a man, wanted to join. However, I was not allowed to join because . . . I couldn't give birth to children. They talked seriously about how to bring up children and how to continue working after having children . . . Not only these things, but also everything was upside down.

4. The students were asked to illustrate the story on the walls of the art room.

Students continued this part of the project throughout the weekend, late into the night. Through illustrations of their story, students expressed each of the themes they had experienced in America up to that point: diversity, government, and technology. However, each theme was interpreted and expressed creatively, as a merge between their own cultural experience, the new cultural experiences, what they were thinking and what they were feeling.

The resulting story and mural symbolized their own confusion in a country where many things were the same as in their own, but in reverse! In the story, women wore trousers, men wore skirts; in the Center's program most professors and persons of responsibility were women, in contrast to their own country. In the illustration, weaker animals were chasing the strong. The Japanese symbol of a woman as a Christmas cake which becomes stale soon after Christmas was crossed out and replaced by "a bottle of red wine, that improves with age" (a phrase they had learned during their trip to the wine country). Diversity was expressed through illustrations of men dancing together, expressing their experiences visiting San Francisco's diverse ethnic and cultural communities, such as the gay community. As they began to stretch

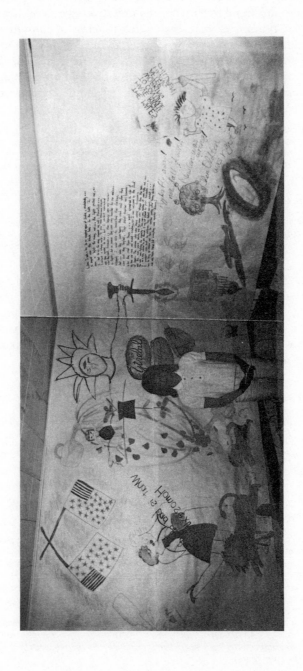

their own cultural boundaries, they wrote, upside down, "What's so bad about homosexuality?" Everything was in reverse: apples were falling upward from the trees, the Statue of Liberty's lamp was upside down; the government themes of "Liberty, Equality, Fraternity" were represented, mirror image and upside down.

Evaluation of the mural in terms of the objective aspects of themes studied would reckon it trivial, if not irrelevant. Evaluation in terms of cultural acquisition on the part of its creators would reckon it a success. Even the composition itself expressed a bridge to the American culture through its eclectic and somewhat controversial content, its broad strokes and spatial organization. At a program evaluation meeting in Japan, Japanese professors observed the effects of cultural acquisition on the participants' behavior. One student reported:

During the questions and answers, we all realized the American utterance style in front of all the professors. Once a question was made by a professor, we answered and gave our opinions, one after another, without break. We did it very naturally. Each of us wanted to say our own opinion. But this utterance style surprised the professors. One of them said to us, "Within a month you gained one of the American styles completely. I'm very surprised. I appreciate it" (Nonaka, 1983).

The professor in charge of the meeting similarly reported:

All the teachers who attended the meeting were impressed with the distinct development in their personality as well as the improvement of their language ability. They were willing to talk, their responses were so prompt, as they had much to say. The effects of the seminar on them were so great that it can be said it resulted in an almost revolutionary change in their mind (Shimada, 1983).

In Chapter 2, discussion of the definitions of culture ended with the idea that culture is, in part, a symbolic process, in which the acquirer creates meaning. As we saw in Chapter 3, meaning can not occur independently of one's previous experience, which includes cultural experience. Meaning, then, hinges on a *synthesis* between the old and the new. The idea of synthesis brings us into the philosophical perspective of how culture is acquired.

Philosophical perspective

Cultural acquisition and change can also be viewed from a philosophical perspective. Marx suggests that cultural change is a socio-historical, dialectic process in which the new product (i.e., change) is the result of a synthesis between the old and the new. Hegel referred to this as thesis-antithesis-synthesis.

Luria's 1930 study of previously isolated villages in Soviet Central Asia illustrates cultural change as a socio-historical process which may change internal ways of thinking, or "forms of consciousness" as he puts it:

The non-technical economy (gardening, cotton-raising, animal husbandry) was replaced by more complex economic systems; there was a sharp increase in the communication with the cities when new people appeared in the villages; collective economy with joint planning and with joint organization of prediction radically changed the previous economic activity; extensive educational and propaganda work intruded on the traditional views which previously had been determined by the simpler life of the village; a large network of schools designed to liquidate illiteracy was introduced to a large portion of population and, in the course of a few years, the residents of these villages were included in a system of educational institutions, and at the same time were introduced to a kind of theoretical activity which had previously not existed in those areas... *All of these events placed before psychology a fundamental question. Did these changes lead only to changes in the contents of conscious life or did they change the forms of consciousness as well?* (Luria, 1971). (*My italics*).

Cultural change is viewed as a socio-historical process and as the response to an integrated network of experiences. Like the empirical studies, this philosophical perspective seems to suggest that one-shot activities and discrete exercises would have little effect on culture learning within second language, foreign language and bilingual programs. This notion of change has its roots in Marx's thesis of life as an historical, dialectic process: man has no fixed nature but is constantly reacting to and integrating new situations to *create* the present state of existence. Existence, for Marx, is a dynamic state.

As individuals express their life, so they are ... men, developing their material production and their material intercourse alter, along with this their real existence, their thinking and the products of their thinking (Marx and Engels, 1970).

This idea of acquisition and change as a dialectic process in which the old experience and the new experience react to and respond with each other is not new to the literature in psychology, anthropology or education. However, the implications have not been widely applied to student responses to culture learning in second language, foreign language and bilingual programs. In these programs students' home cultures come in contact with and must respond to different cultures. According to the above theory, the products of learning would reflect a merge and synthesis between the two. The language and cultural seminar for university women described in the previous section illustrated such a synthesis. Repeated exposure to the same messages and learner response as a cultural merge pervaded each activity, from formal language classes to art and play activities. Even cooking and meals in terms of ingredients, preparation, and serving reflected a synthesis between Japan and America. According to the evaluation meeting, a form of culture change resulted. The following example, though somewhat more simplistic, also illustrates learner response as a cultural merge. In one ESL summer program for Japanese university students at Stanford University, another instructor and myself organized several language classes around the use of American measurements. One integrated unit used the topic of foods to form the background content. Students wrote their favorite recipes using American measurement equivalents. Most of the resulting recipes were Japanese dishes. Students compiled a class recipe book, and prepared one dish to be shared in class. They also made and ate American ice-cream, measuring each ingredient. This activity was directed by the other instructor, who was male. The recipe used was his grandfather's. The male domination of this cooking activity led to interesting class discussion on cultural roles in cooking. Finally, students synthesized their experience while focusing on use of the conditional structure in English. Students responded to the following question: "If you could have dinner with anyone in the world, who would you have dinner with and why? Describe the food, the place and the atmosphere you would want. Note the merge between the Japanese and American cultures in the response of one female student:

If I could have dinner with anyone in the world, I would eat with Rhett Butler in *Gone with the Wind* because he is my ideal lover as well as husband.

I would like to have dinner at a restaurant in the trading center at Kobe.

The night veil is falling down and is surrounding us. Someone is playing the piano. It is so calm and quiet. We are smiling at each other.

I would like to have such a date with him.

A male student wrote:

I would like to have dinner with Masao Kunihiro who is a famous Japanese anthropologist because I am interested in the differences between Japan and America. He tells about it from the point of view of cultural anthropology. It is very interesting for me. I would like to have dinner at the top of the Empire State Building, looking down at New York city. I would like to talk with him about Japan and America while listening to jazz music.

Each of the responses reflects a cultural merge in the content as well as the environment envisaged; clearly, something Japanese, something American, and something individual.

In contrast, educators generally strive to elicit objective responses to the new culture. An ideal response is often considered to be one which sees the culture from the native's point of view. Language and Bilingual Educators are not alone. Within education in general, subjectivity has become a dirty word which tends to undermine scientific inquiry. In programs dealing with culture, the aim is usually to avoid biased observations which result from interpreting the new culture through the learner's own cultural perspective; therefore, objective reporting is preferred. While such a strategy may be valuable for cultural description, it is doubtful that it will promote culture learning in the sense of expanding the learner's *own* repertoire of experiences to become culturally versatile. To repeat once again, "As people express their lives, so they are."

When is the prime time to transmit and acquire cultural learnings?

Language educators have often been concerned with the question of an optimal age to acquire languages, because of its relevance in curriculum planning. The question of an optimal age to acquire cultural learnings would have similar relevance. Is there a prime time for acquiring cultural learnings for the purpose of developing crosscultural understanding?

Early childhood

The literature in cognitive psychology suggests that early childhood is the most essential period for basic cognitive development. Some psychologists even suggest that a child's general intelligence and personality are formed during the first few months of life; others, by the age of seven. Some basic levels of representation in the brain and category prototypes may occur in childhood. A study of how pariah children have school failure and illiteracy illustrates the importance of childhood experiences. Learning to read involves perceptual learnings.

Many children reverse their letters when first learning how to write. Careful attention must be paid to differences in rotation, line-to-line curve . . . in order to make the proper distinctions between letters which signal differences in word form and meaning. We develop these skills and store them deep in our nervous system. The eye apparently learns just what to look for and orients only when a drastically misshapen form appears . . . Some Black children do not permanently develop the essential skills for letter differentiation . . . Most children have trouble with rotation and line-curve transformations at age five. By age seven most children have mastered these transformations. However, Black children I tested at twelve years of age showed a mixed range in these skills; those who could read performed well, and those who could not read performed very poorly, scoring below younger Black children on the same test (McDermott, 1974, p. 95).

While learning not to read, Black children are learning a cultural association: reading is something to turn off to. Print may be selectively avoided. This is not just a learning block; it is a learning in its own right.

According to the above discussion, many patterns of perception may occur in early childhood. Therefore, the influence of cultural experience on general perception, in terms of the categories discussed in Chapter 3, may be greatest in early childhood. This would suggest that instruction aimed at developing cultural versatility in these terms might *most effectively* be incorporated into the early years of schooling. However, perceptual modification occurs throughout life.

Adolescence

The optimum time for cultural acquisition depends upon what is being acquired. While selective perceptual patterns and basic levels of representation may be optimally transmitted during childhood, other aspects of culture such as identification and group affiliation may optimally be acquired during adolescence, as the learner enters a biological stage of transition to adulthood. In *Identity, Youth and Crisis*, Erikson suggests that identity is the critical crisis of youth. The end of the adolescent period is marked by a sense of identity (Erikson, 1968).

Initiation of Arunta, Dinka and Jewish males all occur at puberty. High school girls are initiated into sororities during adolescence. These initiations represent a change and consolidation of identity. Lambert and Klineberg's crosscultural study of children also showed that attitudes towards others, (i.e., outgroups) changed more during adolescence (age 12–13) than at any other time (Lambert and Klineberg, 1966).

It has long been observed that children before puberty acquire native-like accents in foreign language more frequently than those after puberty. These observations have been interpreted biologically: a postulated language acquisition device related to certain areas of the brain becomes fixed at puberty (Penfield, 1978; Lenneberg, 1967). However, experimental studies which control the learning conditions and appropriateness of instruction to adults and children respectively, do not show inferior pronunciation among adults (cf. discussion on optimal age in Robinson (1978a), p. 4). What, then, accounts for our observations that adults do, in fact, exhibit foreign accents more frequently than children under the age of puberty? This observation may also be interpreted in terms of identity consolidation during adolescence rather than biological fixation. Losing one's own accent and acquiring another may involve modifying one's identity: "one of the basic modes of identification by the self and others—the way we sound" (Guiora *et al.*, 1972).

All of the above examples suggest that adolescence is a critical period for consolidation of cultural identity. Therefore, junior high school may be a particularly relevant time for cultural instruction aimed at developing positive attitudes towards and identification with other people. This may be an optimal time for what language educators have called broadening student understanding and lessening insularity (cf. Robinson, 1981).

Any discussion on optimal ages must conclude with a word of caution. "Optimal" refers to the time at which something may be most easily acquired. While perceptual patterns may be more easily acquired in childhood, and group affiliation in adolescence, perceptual patterns and affiliations can be modified throughout life.

Conclusion

This chapter ends with four simple principles. First, analyses of case studies across cultures shows that cultural transmission and acquisition is multi-modal, regarding specific cultural messages as well as complex learnings such as world view. This suggests that the more modes stimulated, the more efficient the acquisition (i.e., the less time in which something is learned and the longer it is remembered). In contrast, schooling, especially higher education, is dominated by verbal, analytical transmission. **Implication:** support experiential, multi-modal instruction at all levels.

Second, cultural learnings are acquired within an integrated context. Integrated contexts afford repeated exposure to the same learning or set of learnings. Language may be viewed as a complex set of cultural learnings. **Implication:** avoid discrete-item instruction, within and across exercises, both linguistic and cultural.

Third, second cultural acquisition involves cultural change. From a Marxist philosophical perspective, cultural change is a dialectic process in which learners react to an all-encompassing set of socio-historical conditions. (Change affects not only external institutions and behaviors, but people's minds.) The result is a synthesized meaning, created by the learner, who merges past cultural experience with the new. **Implication:** Encourage subjectivity that is related to the subject matter. Elicit a synthesis between the learner's home cultural experience and the new.

Fourth, the optimal age for cultural transmission and acquisition depends on what is being transmitted. Perceptual patterns appear to be naturally acquired during early childhood. Identity and group affiliation appear to be consolidated during adolescence. **Implication:** in planning instruction aimed at developing crosscultural understanding, consider the ages at which particular goals are most easily fulfilled. Adolescence may be the most efficient time to promote learner identification with culturally diverse groups.

Notes

1 Some messages may be transmitted through telepathy. However, since telepathy still remains without complete scientific explanation, it will not be elaborated in this chapter. At this stage the implications of apparent telepathic practices, such as "singing a tribe member back" among Australian Aborigines, are difficult to apply to a strategy for culture learning.

Chapter 5

How do cultural learnings affect the perception of other people?

No one denies that both present cognitive processes and past learning history determine social behavior. That is, a person's past experience influences his interpretation of any current situation and shapes his responses to it; but the interpretation and perceptual view of the current situation are major determinants of how the individual responds (Freedman *et al.*, p. 15).

Introduction

In the last chapter we saw how cultural learnings are acquired. This chapter focuses on how these cultural learnings influence the perception of other people. Developing crosscultural understanding involves perceiving members of different cultural groups positively. By understanding the basic principles of person perception, and the natural effects of one's own cultural experience and learnings on perceiving other people, unproductive explanations of crosscultural misunderstandings as prejudice or even just differences may be replaced with productive methods of avoiding misunderstandings and stimulating positive perceptions of other people. How we perceive other people affects how we behave toward them and how they, in turn, behave toward us.

In Chapter 3 we saw how experience within a culture influenced perception in general, i.e., what we select to see from a visual array, how we organize it, how we think about it, and how we interpret it. Similarly, experience within a culture affects how we perceive other people. Experience acts like a dynamic movie director inside the actor, who encourages the actor to interpret other people and their environment in particular ways and to act accordingly. In psychological terms, people develop *schemas* through which to perceive, organize and interpret social events and people, just as with visual arrays. Cues and values associated with cues affect first impressions. These first impressions affect subsequent evaluations of other people, their behaviors and related situations, which in turn affect how other people are treated. To the extent that members of a given culture tend to share in these schemas, cues and values, cultural learnings and experiences influence how people perceive others.

This chapter suggests that *cultural misunderstandings are a function of perceptual mismatches* between people of different cultures: mismatches in schemas, cues, values and interpretations. While actual cultural differences contribute to many such mismatches, many perceived, apparent differences are a function of errors in cognitive processing. Some psychologists refer to these errors as cognitive biases.

The first part of this chapter is concerned with the basic principles of social perception and their possible relationship to cultural experience. The second part is concerned with misunderstandings from the perspective of actual differences as well as cognitive biases. The last section summarizes the principles that emerge and their implications for educational programs aimed at developing positive social perceptions and interactions among people from different cultures.

How does cultural experience influence social perception?

Affiliation is determined to some extent by one's expectations about interactions with other people and by one's knowledge of them (Freedman *et al.*, p. 88).

Cues

Three types of cue influence how people perceive others: "the person himself or herself, the person's behavior, and the context or situation the person is in" (*Ibid.*, p. 97). Experience within a particular culture familiarizes cultural actors with these cues, and thus influences affiliation.

Physical cues

Various aspects of physical appearance influence how people perceive others, particularly physique, height, facial features and clothing. Overall physical attractiveness is one of the most important factors in first impressions. As we saw in the last chapter, cultural experience influences aesthetic values of what is attractive. For example, to the Dinka of the Sudan, extraction of the lower teeth enhances one's beauty. Moreover, tooth extraction is a familiar sight among the Dinka and is associated with cultural affiliation. According to the quote at the beginning of this chapter, it would seem to follow that a person with the lower teeth in place might be considered less attractive among the Dinka. Similarly, thin lips may be a sign of beauty in one culture, thick lips in another; a slight physique may be more familiar and more positively identified in one culture; a heavy physique in another. If affiliation is determined to some extent by one's expectations of the person, including expectations of appearance, then cultural familiarity with particular aspects of physical appearance would appear to influence positive affiliation. Similarly, lack of familiarity might inhibit affiliation and result in negative impressions. Aspects of physical appearance which are culturally familiar also tend to reflect similarity among group members. Psychological research suggests that perceived similarity increases liking.

Behavioral cues

Just as with physical cues, cultural experience contributes to one's familiarity with as well as similarity of behavioral cues, verbal cues, para-verbal cues, and non-verbal cues. While the relationship of cultural experience to these cues has been treated elsewhere, a few examples are in order (cf. Robinson, 1981, chapter 4). Verbal cues refer to syntax, phonology, lexicon and even the frequency with which certain meanings are conveyed. One study by Zajonc (1968) suggested that familiarity with a particular lexicon influences positive perception of these words.

Subjects were shown a number of Turkish words, and some of the words were shown many more times than others. (In other studies, nonsense syllables and Chinese words were used.) Afterward. the subjects were asked to guess the meanings of the words. There was a strong tendency for them to give positive meanings to the words they had seen more often (Zajonc, 1968).

Clearly, experience within a culture affects one's familiarity with all verbal cues. Analogously, it would appear that the more similar someone else's language was perceived to be to one's own, the more positive the perception of the language and the user, and the reverse. Different languages also use extra-verbal cues to convey different meanings. Extra-verbal cues refer to audible signs that are part of the verbal system, such as speech intonation, stress, pitch, volume, speed, and length of speech and pauses.

What is apparently the same sign often contains different cultural messages. For example, the degree of speech volume that would convey anger differs for speakers of Japanese and Italian. In one culture loudness may be interpreted as abruptness; in another culture softness may be interpreted as timidity. The degree of volume that designates the value "loud" itself differs across cultures (Robinson, 1981, p. 41).

Experience within a culture affects the meaning and value associated with extra-verbal cues. Non-verbal cues refer to the meanings associated with the use of time, the organization of space, the way people move. For example, the same gesture may cue different attitudes across cultures. The act of looking down by a student while being spoken to by a Mexican teacher might occasion the teacher's positive perception of the student. In this case, looking down might signal respect, which is highly valued. The same act might occasion a negative perception on the part of an American teacher. Looking down might signal inattention or guilt. Looking the teacher in the eye would instead cue a positive perception (Olguin, 1978). Positive perceptions among people from different cultures would thus be influenced by (1) the degree of similarity in the cues and their meanings, and (2) the listener's knowledge of what the speaker's cues mean from the speaker's cultural perspective. Without such knowledge and accuracy of expectation, an American might perhaps perceive a Japanese speaker as overly timid, an Italian as overly pushy. Similarly, an American might appear overly aggressive or angry to a Japanese.

Person perception becomes more difficult when we try to infer an individual's feelings and emotions from external cues. Some researchers have tried to identify certain emotional cues as universally recognizable. In one study, subjects were asked to match emotionally-cued pictures to stories (Ekman and Friesen, 1971). However, the stories reflected highly contrasting emotions, such as sadness at the death of a child and happiness. Even if "happy" in all settings were to be cued by laughter, the reverse would not necessarily always be true. For example, the Japanese generally smile and giggle to express happiness; however, smiles and giggles may also cue embarrassment just as frequently. Cultural norms differ not only in the cues for particular emotions, but also in the amount of emotion expressed at all, and the amount appropriate within different contexts. Without a familiar context, non-verbal cues are at best incomprehensible, and at worst, misinterpreted. Persons are perceived more accurately when verbal and non-verbal cues are available.

In general, people are perceived much more accurately when visual information is available as well as purely verbal messages (Archer and Akert, 1977).

The above has important implications for second and foreign language programs, as well as other cultural studies, in which target cultural persons are often portrayed either through a written account or a film. Here again, the idea of multi-modal instruction, discussed in Chapter 4, is reinforced.

Schemas

Schemas refer to cognitive structures through which people interpret information. In other words, schemas contribute in large part to the interpretation and meaningfulness of particular contexts. People interpret events as well as other persons through them. They are like theories: we see other people as we expect to according to our theories, rather than simply in terms of what they actually do or are.

Person schemas

Person schemas may focus on particular people such as George Washington, or on particular kinds of people, such as professors or intelligent people. Person schemas are structures about people which include traits that are grouped together. For example, people who are perceived to be helpful are also perceived to be sincere and popular. Similarly, people who are considered to be scientific are also considered to be determined and reliable. Person schemas are widely shared among people with a common background and therefore influence the traits that go together in a given person schema. In particular, cultural experience influences the traits that go together in a role schema. For example, the person schema for a high school teacher in Japan may group together traits such as intelligent, male, high status, authority and humility. In an American public school the person schema for a teacher may not include high status or humility, while intelligent may be grouped with different traits.

Event schemas

An event schema is like a script: it anticipates or suggests a particular sequence of events within a particular setting, which may be characterized by particular roles and behaviors of participating actors. In the psychological literature, a script is a standard sequence of behavior over a period of time. However, what is a standard sequence within a situation varies from culture to culture (cf. Robinson, 1981, p. 45). Experience within a particular culture clearly influences each aspect of event schemas. Compare for example a business dinner in an upper middle class American home, Japanese home, and Mexican home. In the American situation, either the host or hostess might open the door and both would be expected to greet the guests. In some cases guests might bring a gift of wine, candy or flowers. While it would not be necessary, it would not be inappropriate. Wine or candy would likely be opened and shared during or after the meal; flowers would be openly displayed. In an American home, the guests might be expected to intermingle relatively equally. All male guests would likely engage in handshaking. There would be few non-verbal or verbal markers of relative role status, even though their roles did differ in relative status. The hostess might have help serving the meal or might serve it herself. Guests would wait for the hostess to be seated and for all to be served before commencing the meal. The hostess would enjoy the meal with her guests, and the conversation during the meal could involve both male and female guests.

In Mexico, guests would most likely be greeted by a formal servant. Gifts are not expected in this situation. Conversation would probably be initiated by the guest of higher status. The meal would be served by servants, and the hostess would also enjoy the meal with the guests. Conversation would be more divided by sexes. Within such a context, a hostess who served the meal might be perceived as less gracious and the family of lower status. A woman who initiated a business conversation with a male guest might be perceived as aggressive.

In Japan the hostess would probably open the door and invite the guests into the house. Guests would likely present a gift, *omiagi* to the hostess, which would be acknowledged and then put away. Generally, it would not be opened during the guests' stay. Opening of a gift in the presence of the giver is culturally inappropriate. Shortly after, the host would greet the guests. From this point on, the hostess would be engaged in serving the guests; she would most likely not participate in conversation. Guests would not wait for the hostess to sit down to commence to eat. In fact, the hostess might not eat with the guests at all.

In each situation above, positive perceptions of the event as well as the people involved would be occasioned by behaviors that matched the respective script.

Evaluation of others

Social psychologists suggest that evaluation is the major dimension of person perception. Evaluations of other people reflect the perception of particular traits, their associated values, the degree of perceived similarity, and the projection of self with regard to the target person. The resulting evaluation constitutes a first impression of the target person.

Central traits theory

The psychological literature suggests that some traits are inherently more meaningful than others. These inherently more meaningful traits are called "central traits." Evaluation of a person is determined in large part by the degree of positivity perceived in the central traits.

The pair of traits warm-cold appears to be associated with a great number of other characteristics, whereas the pair polite-blunt, under most circumstances, is associated with fewer (Freedman *et al.*, 1981).

Cultural experience influences the value associated with particular traits. The traits that would be central vary considerably across cultures. In contrast to the above quote, it is likely that to the Japanese, the pair of traits, polite-blunt, would be associated with a greater number of characteristics than the pair warm-cold. An American perceived as warm but impolite might make a negative impression to the Japanese. Conversely, a Japanese perceived as cold but polite might make a negative impression on an American. To an American, cold is included in a person schema which associates cold with a negative value, as in bad or undesirable.

Projections of self

Another factor in evaluating others is how one feels about oneself. We tend to project feelings about ourselves onto others. For example, people who are threatened view others as more threatening. In one study, subjects who were liable to be drafted and those who were not, were shown pictures of military men. Those who were liable to be drafted described the military men as more threatening and more authoritarian than the other subjects (Bartlett, 1932).

The educational literature has long acknowledged and addressed the relationship of self to achievement in general. However, the notion that people project their own feelings onto the perception of other people has particular relevance to bilingual, second language and foreign language programs, aimed at developing positive perceptions among people of different cultural groups. Currently, the literature on bilingual education stresses the importance of developing the minority child's self concept. However, the literature does not deal with the importance of a positive self-concept among mainstream children in pluralistic settings. According to the above notion, mainstream children in a bilingual classroom who felt inadequate in their understanding of Spanish might project their feelings onto native Spanish speakers in their classroom. Similarly, foreign language classrooms have frequently been cited as embarrassing situations for adolescents and adults. While student embarrassment has been acknowledged, little if anything has been done to decrease the embarrassment; rather, learner embarrassment is anticipated and accepted. Psychological research on social perception would suggest that more emphasis be placed on structuring tasks that develop a positive self-concept among all learners in bilingual, multicultural and foreign language programs.

Similarity

How people perceive other people is influenced by the degree of similarity perceived. As mentioned earlier, cultural experience influences which cues and schema will become familiar and anticipated. Cues which are familiar tend to be those which are similar. Numerous studies have shown that perceived similarity influences liking (cf. Byrne, 1961; Byrne and Nelson, 1964; Newcomb, 1961).

On practically every dimension except perhaps personality characteristics . . . people who are similar tend to like each other (Freedman et al., p. 208).

The implication for programs aimed at developing positive affiliation would be to focus on similarities. The influence of dissimilarities on crosscultural misunderstandings will be discussed in the second part of this chapter.

First impressions

Once people evaluate other people, these evaluations contribute to first impressions, which tend to be made quickly, on the basis of very limited information. However, once first impressions are made, they are difficult to change, due to a variety of cognitive biases. These first impressions affect not only how people perceive others, but also how they behave toward them. That is, if, for some reason, John Smith negatively perceives Jose Gonzalez, John is going to behave towards Jose in such a way that Jose will not like John, or else John will tend to avoid Jose altogether (cf. Newcombe, 1961). The importance of first impressions on subsequent perceptions of other people suggests that bilingual, foreign language and multicultural programs pay particular attention to the way in which target cultural instruction is *introduced*, so that positive evaluations and positive first impressions result.

How do crosscultural misunderstandings occur?
Actual dissimilarity of cues and events

It is important to understand how misunderstandings and negative evaluations occur, so that instruction aimed at developing positive evaluations among people from different cultures may learn what pitfalls to avoid.

If perceived similarity contributes to positive evaluations of other people, it is plausible that perceived dissimilarity and mismatching cues and schemas would contribute to negative impressions of people from cultures different from one's own.

A Sydney study supported the negative effects of perceived dissimilarity on student impressions of people from foreign countries. In the study, 156 students comprising the entire seventh grade population of one school responded to five open-ended questions involving student interest in foreign countries and impressions of foreign peoples (Robinson, 1981, chapter 5). All questions were scattered throughout a general student background questionnaire. One question sought impressions about foreign people in general: "What impressions do you have of foreign peoples? Name the nationality you are referring to." Another question sought impressions about foreign people they had met: "Have you ever met or spoken to anyone from a foreign country? If so, what were your impressions?" While the majority of all impressions were positive or neutral, 41% were negative. One-third of all negative impressions involved the ethnic group most represented in the area surrounding the school after Anglo-Australians: the Italians. (The remaining responses were spread over 37 other groups.) More than half the negative responses toward Italians involved perceived dissimilarity of habits, e.g., "don't like the foods they eat, smell of garlic, always wearing black, morbid" and dissimilarity of verbal and extra-verbal cues, e.g., "always shouting, don't like their accent, arrogant, abrupt" (*Ibid.*, p. 54).

The studies of Gumperz, Jupp and Roberts (1979) also support the idea that perceived dissimilarity of speech conventions and mismatching interpretations contributes to crosscultural misunderstandings. The researchers suggest that communication between people from different ethnic groups breaks down due to three main types of differences:

(1) Different cultural assumptions about the situation and about appropriate behavior and intentions within it.
(2) Different ways of structuring information or an argument in a conversation.
(3) Different ways of speaking; the use of a different set of unconscious linguistic conventions (such as tone of voice) to emphasize, to signal connections and logic, and to imply the significance of what is being said in terms of overall meaning and attitudes (Gumperz *et al.*, 1979, p. 5).

To the above, I would add:

(4) Different ways of interacting: reciprocal versus non-reciprocal forms of conversation.

Different cultural assumptions

Gumperz *et al.* illustrate the onset of communication difficulties when a conversation begins with unshared assumptions about the purpose of the interaction. The interaction is an interview between a British social worker and Mr. Aziz, who has recently lost his job. Mr. Aziz originally came from India and has worked in Britain since 1959. Mr. Aziz has been seeking unemployment benefits for several months to no avail. However, he does not want supplementary benefits, which is welfare.

The social worker and Mr. Aziz start with different points of view about the interview. The social worker is concerned with the *facts* of what Mr. Aziz has done and compares these facts with the correct procedure. He wants to establish where the discrepancy is and why the system has gone wrong. Then he can help Mr. Aziz. Mr. Aziz, on the other hand, is concerned with projecting his "*needs* and his *feelings*." His major concern is that he wants the benefits he is entitled to and has paid for, and that he resents being crossexamined or laughed at when he asks for such benefits (Gumperz *et al.*, p. 16).

The social worker incorrectly assumes that Mr. Aziz does not understand the distinction between unemployment benefits and social welfare, and thus "deliberately tries to simplify things by using the single term 'social security' to cover both types of benefits." This reflects a stereotyped assumption about Mr. Aziz, and underestimates his knowledge of the system. Mr. Aziz, on the other hand, not only distinguishes between the two, but feels entitled to unemployment benefits, while he would be too ashamed to accept welfare. Since the social worker continually asks Mr. Aziz to describe the steps he has taken to obtain social security, Mr. Aziz is confused as to how to answer, and keeps expressing his shame when he thinks the social worker is referring to welfare. "Mr. Aziz is aware that people are quick to accuse immigrants of sponging off the Social Services" (*Ibid.*). Instead of receiving both the empathy and the help he sought, Mr. Aziz leaves the interview frustrated and humiliated. The social worker, on the other hand, perceives Mr. Aziz to be confused about the facts and remains unsure whether he ever applied for social security benefits at all.

I asked graduate students of Bilingual Education at the University of Santa Clara to observe and report on how inter-ethnic communication breaks down in school interactions due to different cultural assumptions. One student reported on a school conference. The teacher had sent a note home requesting that the parents come into the school to have a conference regarding the child, who was Vietnamese. To the teacher's surprise and annoyance, the oldest son in the family appeared at the school instead of the parents. The student reporting explains how such a difference could lead to communication breakdown and negative perceptions:

The teacher wants to talk about the student's problems. She expects to see the parents, as she assumes that they are the responsible party. In Vietnamese homes the father is responsible. However, if the father is dead, (e.g., killed in war, etc.) the oldest son, not the mother, takes over. Without knowing this, the teacher might be annoyed, wondering where the mother is and if she is concerned about her child.

In such a situation the teacher might also fail to continue the conference with the oldest son or fully disclose the problem, feeling such would be inappropriate. As a result, the home might never receive an understanding of the child's problems in school, and consequently the child might not receive help from the home in that area.

Different ways of structuring information and arguments in a conversation

In a formal interview or professional conversation, Americans generally expect speakers to come to the point. Objectivity and directness are positively valued; speakers are cautioned against beating around the bush. This illustrates a conventional style of rhetoric in American formal speech. Mismatching conventions in structuring information and arguments may lead to negative perceptions of the speech partners. Such conventions "influence whether a person sounds relevant, logical and concise to a listener." Three examples of Asian-English conventions are given which "tend to destroy a sense of logic and relevance for an English-English speaker." (In their analyses, "Asian-English" refers to the speech of English speakers from India and Pakistan.)

(a) In English-English, a key topic word is often repeated in order to establish the immediate relevance of the answer or comment. This often rhythmic repetition of a key word or phrase seldom happens with Asian-English speakers.

(b) In Asian-English, it is customary to repeat some part of what the speaker has just said, although it may not be relevant to the point being made in reply. This can give a sense of being repetitive or inconsistent.

(c) In some Asian-English styles of speaking, too direct a response is avoided. The speaker responds first of all in a general sort of way, only moving later to his important specific points. The English-English style of logic is the opposite, and this means that the English-English listener may well have switched off before the important point occurs, particularly if the differences under (a) and (b) are also present. (*Ibid.*)

Students at the University of Santa Clara also observed and reported on different ways of structuring information that contribute to negative perceptions and misunderstandings of people from other cultures. One student reported that, at a parent conference between an Anglo teacher and a Chicano parent, the teacher mentioned that the parent's daughter was often late to school.

The parent explained the home situation and the child's work schedules. Then the parent finally acknowledged the problem saying that she'd take care of it. By then, the teacher was impatient and tired of all the parent's "excuses."

Another student, herself a teacher, observed her own annoyance at what she had perceived to be needlessly long phone calls. She called home to report what she called "bad behavior."

I wanted to describe the problem and wanted support and the parents' word that they would resolve the problem. Many times I am long engaged on the phone. Mexican parents go to the extreme of thanking me and promising to help. But all I really expect is a quick release from the phone and a "thank you."

Misunderstanding between Japanese and American speakers are also influenced by different ways of structuring information. The American value of directness is contrasted with the Japanese value of maintaining harmony. Japanese use a variety of conventions to avoid direct disagreement. For example, when invited to a function they are unable to attend, Japanese speakers may accept the invitation rather than directly refusing the offer; it is more appropriate simply not to attend than to directly refuse the invitation. Responses to yes/no questions tend to be in the affirmative. For example, students who did not have their homework might respond to the question, "Don't you have your homework?" or "You don't have your homework, do you?" with "yes." "Yes" would indicate that the listener is in agreement with the speaker's statement, i.e., "Yes, I agree with you. I don't have my homsework." A direct question is rarely answered with a simple "no." The phrase *chigaimasu*, meaning, "it is different" is frequently employed. Japanese speakers structure arguments to avoid direct refusal and direct confrontation. To a Japanese who is expecting similar forms of arguments, the directness of American conversation often appears rude and inconsiderate. An American, on the other hand, often becomes annoyed at the confusing rhetoric and unnecessary beating around the bush of Japanese speakers.

Different ways of speaking

In the beginning section on behavioral cues, we saw the cultural influences on verbal, extra-verbal, and non-verbal cues. We also saw the effects of familiarity with cues on expectations. Different extra-verbal cues, i.e., the meanings associated with tone of voice, stress, pitch, and rhythm (also referred to as paralinguistics or prosody), are important causes of communication breakdown. The effects of different ways of speaking among speakers of British English and Asian-English have been summarized as follows:

What can confuse English people and lead to irritation

(1) Certain uses of high or low pitched voice and loudness, e.g., Raising voice in "No" to contradict.

(2) Lack of stress, e.g., Not marking clearly the difference between *last* week and *this* week.

(3) Use of Yes/No, e.g., Saying "yes" but not meaning that you agree.

(4) Lack of cohesive features in discourse so that the Asian speaker appears boring or confused, e.g., misleading intonation patterns, unclear pronoun references.

(5) Wrong use of turn-taking, e.g., persistently interrupting in the middle of the English speaker's utterance.

What can confuse Asian people and lead to irritation

(1) Tone of voice: high pitch or stress on *particular* words. This can sound emotional and impolite, e.g., when an English speaker wants to explain or emphasize a certain point.

(2) Apparent not listening, e.g., in longer chunks of discourse the English speaker may switch off, or change the subject.

(3) Many forms of inexplicit or indirect statements and questions.

(4) Apologetic or polite and repetitive uses of English.

(*Ibid.*)

Students at the University of Santa Clara observed a variety of differences in ways of speaking which contributed to misunderstandings among students and teachers from different cultural backgrounds. The following are three examples of student observations.

(1) Speech partners: Adolescent Black Child and Middle-Aged Anglo Teacher.
I have witnessed the refusal of a teacher to speak to a student concerning unfavorable behavior because of the student's usage of certain vernacular and "nonstandard" English.

(2) Speech partners: Mexican-American Child and Anglo Teacher.
English uses 3 levels of pitch for normal conversation and a 4th level for anger, excitement, etc. Spanish uses 2 levels for normal conversation and the 3rd is for excitement. Young Spanish-speaking children in a class may misinterpret a teacher as yelling, angry or excited when it is not the case.

(3) Speech partners: Mexican-American Teacher and Filipino Teacher.
In conversing with the Filipino teacher next door, I have often felt that her slowness of speech indicated her incompetence or "newness" as a teacher. Her speech is slow and she uses many questions and responses involving uncertainty. Through this class I have come to realize that I'm misinterpreting her on the basis of speech differences. Actually she is being humble.

Different ways of interacting: reciprocity of communication

Experience within a culture also affects learned patterns of interaction in a conversation. Is the interaction reciprocal? For example, is it appropriate for speakers to speak the same amount of time a conversation? My own research suggests that cultural experience affects the degree to which speech will be reciprocal or non-reciprocal. The following grid illustrates four dimensions of speech which may be either reciprocal/(equal) or non-reciprocal/(unequal):

Dimensions of Reciprocal and Non-reciprocal Speech

	TIME	SPEECH INITIATION	INTERACTIVE STYLE	CONTENT
RECIPROCAL	equal	partners are *equal* in asking questions and initiating speech	*zig zag*: speech is back and forth in short chunks	*responsive*: partner 2's speech refers to what partner 1 has said
NON-RECIPROCAL	unequal	one partner is dominant in initiating speech & asking questions; the other partner generally responds	each partner speaks in long chunks without interruption	*unresponsive*: each partner's speech is independent of previous speaker's content, as in monologues.

In the crosscultural training film *Take Two* (IRI, 1982) non-reciprocity of speech initiation and content is illustrated between an American student and a Vietnamese student. An American student is seen trying to befriend a Vietnamese student. In an attempt to keep the conversation going, the American continually asks questions; the Vietnamese responds, often with a "yes" or "no," or with a very short answer, without elaboration or extension. After this conversation filmed in *Take One*, each student is interviewed as to their feelings. The American comments that it was very difficult to converse with the Vietnamese student; the American felt the Vietnamese student was not interested in her, because she never asked the American any questions in return. The Vietnamese student on the other hand felt that the American kept "firing" questions at her, without giving her enough time to respond. (For the American, any pauses after the student's response was uncomfortable.) She was also not accustomed to the American style of elaborating and then asking back. After intervention training, more effective communication occurs in *Take Two*, in which the American pauses after each question and does not jump in with another question until the Vietnamese student has had ample chance to reply. The Vietnamese student has also learned to ask questions back to the American.

Students in my crosscultural communication course within the TESOL Certificate Program, University of California, Berkeley, were asked to observe conversations, and monitor their own, according to the four dimensions of reciprocity described above. One student reported observations from three conversations. She observed that degree of reciprocity, even with speakers from the same culture, differed according to the purpose of the conversation. In one personal conversation, the conversation was non-reciprocal in terms of time, speech initiation, and interactive style: questions were probing, eliciting long responses; however, the content was responsive—each question was related to the previous speaker's reply. In a different conversation, which was primarily "social" in nature, interaction was reciprocal along each dimension. In a third conversation between student and teacher, speech was non-reciprocal except in content responsiveness.

Reciprocity of speech, even within a particular culture, tends to vary according to situation and to speaker. For example, within the American culture, speech may be non-reciprocal among teacher and student, but reciprocal among two teachers. There are also differences between individuals. While intracultural, individual differences do exist, cultural learnings do tend to affect conventional interactive patterns and influence what type of interaction will be expected and considered appropriate within different situations across cultures.

At the Center for Language and Crosscultural Skills, San Francisco, California, several strategies were developed to train Japanese students in reciprocal communication style. In one exercise, students played "the interrupting game" to accustom them to interrupt the speaker. This game was integrated with listening comprehension in *l* versus *r*. The class was divided into two teams. The teacher read a poem to the class, which contained numerous *l* and *r* sounds. In the first half of the exercise, students were instructed to yell-out "excuse me" each time they heard *l*. Each correct response gained a point for their team. However, an incorrect response earned a point for the opposing team. The game was played a second time listening for words containing the *r* sound. In another exercise, students practiced "equal participation" in terms of time, in combination with the goals of reading comprehension and conversation practice. The class was again divided into teams. The class was given a common handout to read. Students were instructed to ask questions to other classmates based on the reading. One point was given for each question related to the reading, each response, and/or each elaboration of another person's response. However, no one person on a given team could speak until each person on their own team had spoken.

In a third exercise, students practiced reciprocal speech in terms of speech initiation, interaction style and content. In a game called "Keep the conversation going," the class was divided into pairs. Each pair had to follow the same format for a designated time period.

Partner A: asks a question.
Partner B: answers, elaborates, asks a related question to Partner A.
Partner A: answers, elaborates, asks a question on the topic to Partner B, and so on.

In the Crosscultural Communication Program at the University of California, Berkeley, TESL students learned the same principles by contrast. They played "Kill the Conversation" in which each student made a list of ten unrelated questions to ask another classmate. The class was divided into pairs. In the first round, Partner A always asked the question. Partner B always responded with as short a response as possible. Partner B was not allowed to elaborate or question Partner B. Following each short response, Partner A asked a different question. In round two, the partners switched roles.

Students within the same program were asked to develop their own strategies to teach both reciprocal and non-reciprocal styles along each dimension above. The use of ethnography as a tool for developing non-reciprocal, in-depth conversations will be discussed in Chapter 6.

In summary, different ways of interacting in terms of reciprocity of communication often cause ineffective if not mis-communication. These types of communication breakdown may be remedied or avoided by two-way training, in which speakers become skilled in both reciprocal and non-reciprocal styles.

Remedying misunderstandings due to actual dissimilarites

In all of the examples throughout this section, actual dissimilarities of cultural assumptions, ways of structuring information, speech conventions, and reciprocity of conversation caused mismatches between what was anticipated, what occurred, and how events were interpreted. While these mismatches cause substantial crosscultural miscommunication, they are perhaps the most easily remedied. These kinds of mismatch result from incorrect expectations of the other speech partner's behavior. Therefore, they may be remedied by knowledge on the part of both speech partners, i.e., knowledge of the diverse cultural assumptions. Effective communication, like miscommunication, is a two-way process requiring two-way treatment. In a conversation, each partner must check the other's purpose and cultural assumptions about the conversation; each must learn about the diverse ways people structure information; each must learn the different meanings associated with different ways of speaking and different forms of interaction; and each must learn to anticipate and engage in reciprocal and non-reciprocal forms of speech.

The idea of effective crosscultural understanding as a two-way process has particular implications for bilingual, second language and foreign language programs. In bilingual education programs, English as a second language is generally required for limited English proficient (LEP) students. However, there is little planned instruction aimed at teaching mainstream monolingual English speakers the language of LEP students with whom they daily interact. Within foreign language programs, communication is also studied from a one-way perspective. One could also debate whether any of these programs generally deal with the four types of communication differences discussed in this chapter.

Each of these programs would benefit from including instruction regarding these kinds of differences, not only from the target language's point of view, but from their own. For example, foreign language students may avoid communication breakdown by learning how their own language and cultural conventions may be misinterpreted, as much as by studying what to appropriately expect from the target culture's point of view. Clearly, learning about cultural differences in speech conventions, ways of structuring arguments, cultural assumptions and interaction patterns has an important role to play in programs aimed at developing positive crosscultural communication. To the extent that such knowledge increases one's familiarity with, and expectations of, another person's communication style, it should lessen perceptual mismatch and decrease misunderstanding due to actual cultural dissimilarities.

Cognitive biases

Knowledge may work particularly well for learners who do not already have an established negative frame of reference regarding members of the target culture. However, once negative impressions are formed, increasing information about the target culture may not be sufficient to change these impressions, remedy misunderstandings, or override certain cognitive biases that perpetuate the perception of apparent differences. A known fact of psychology is that people are not always rational or objective in perceiving and interpreting the behavior of other people. Available information regarding other people is selectively perceived and processed. Several cognitive biases contribute to the perception of apparent differences and crosscultural misunderstandings. These biases include: the human tendency for consistency, the availability of salient or distinctive features, and faulty inferences.

Tendency for consistency

As mentioned earlier, how people evaluate others is influenced by cultural experience. Once impressions are formed, and a frame of reference is established, these evaluations are difficult to change. People have a tendency for consistency.

Attribution theory assumes that we have a need to develop an understanding of predictable relations in order to give stability and meaning to events in our lives. This leads to a reality orientation to the world (Zimbardo and Ruch, 1977).

While this tendency for consistency influences all perception, it is particularly important in person perception.

There is a tendency to view another person as consistent, especially in an evaluative sense . . . The perceivers distort or rearrange information to minimize or eliminate the inconsistency. This may happen to some extent when people perceive objects, but it is particularly strong in person perception (Freedman et al., p. 89).

People tend to interpret the behavior of other people in a way which is consistent with their established frame of reference. In order to maintain consistency, people may reject, discount or distort information that does not fit the established framework. "The deeper a person's commitment to an attitude, the greater his tendency to reject dissonant information" (Aronson, 1972, p. 92).

Hastorf and Cantril report a study which demonstrates how people distort and reject information to maintain their established frame of reference. A football game between Princeton and Dartmouth resulted in one of the roughest games in history, including injuries to star players on both sides. After the game, the researchers showed films of the game to students on each campus. Students were instructed to write down each infraction of the rules, how it started, and who was responsible.

There was a strong tendency for the students to see their own fellow students as victims of illegal aggression, rather than as perpetrators of illegal aggression. ... Princeton students saw fully twice as many violations on the part of the Dartmouth players as the Dartmouth students saw (Hastorf and Cantril, 1954).

The Sydney study of student impressions mentioned earlier also suggests that people interpret information in accordance with their general frame of reference. Student impressions of specific people they had met often differed from general impressions of members of that nationality. In many cases, the same students who indicated having had a positive experience with particular Italians held negative attitudes towards Italians in general.

According to the theories of consistency and stereotyping, a positive experience with and impression of a specific person would not alter the general frame of reference of, say, "Italians." Rather, the latter would alter the interpretation of the former. One might say, for example, "I met an Italian who was nice, but he is an exception." Our general frame of reference would influence our interpretation of the conflicting experience (Robinson, 1981).

In judging other people's behaviors, we may discount certain causes if other plausible causes are present. Typically, we observe the person's behavior or act, and then discount the factors caused by the situation or environment. We use our own past experience to determine how particular situations generally affect people (Kelley, 1972). Judging people from other cultures becomes somewhat more complex and inaccurate: it is difficult to know what to accurately "discount." Let us take the example of a person who commits *Hara Kiri* in Japan and a person who commits suicide in the United States. Both people commit the same behavior, i.e., suicide. However, in evaluating each person's behavior, the factors to be discounted would be quite different. In the United States, it is likely that the behavior would be attributed to the person and his/her personal instability. In Japan, it is likely that the behavior would be attributed to factors in the social or political environment. One's frame of reference regarding another person influences what will be discounted, and what evaluation of an event will result.

In a study by Thibaut and Riecken (1955), subjects were asked to evaluate the same behaviour exhibited by two different people: a high status person and a low-status person. It has been suggested that the frame of reference for high-status people generally includes the notion that they control their behaviors, whereas low-status people are easily influenced by others, i.e., externally motivated. The researchers found that subjects' judgments of different people's behavior coincided with this frame of reference: subjects attributed the low status person's behavior to the outside pressure put on him; subjects attributed the high status person's behaviour to his own desire.

Status characteristics and expectation status theory

Perceived status not only influences evaluation of another person, but the degree to which one chooses to listen to and interact with that person. According to the status characteristic theory, "power and prestige order in a newly constituted group of high and low status members comes to parallel the relative ranking on a status characteristic initially held by members of the group" (Cohen and Roper, 1972). That is, perceived status characteristics about oneself as well as "other" are generalized or diffused to the new situation.

The high status member, expecting to be more competent at the new task, initiates more remarks from the beginning of the interaction and becomes more influential as the members interact. The low status member, expecting to be less competent than the high status member, initiates less at the outset, overevaluating the contribution of the more talkative high status members and underevaluating his own contribution (*Ibid.*).

In order to determine if race were a clear instance of a diffuse status characteristic, Cohen and Roper conducted a series of experiments in which nineteen groups of two black and two white junior high school boys were videotaped while playing the game, "Kill the Bull." All four players in the group had to decide each move cooperatively. After every throw of the dice, the entire group had to decide which direction to go. The group had to evaluate each individual's suggestion to decide where to move. The results were as follows:

In fourteen of nineteen groups . . . we found that a white actor was the more active on the task (*Ibid.*).

In most groups, the white members of the group ignored the comments of the black members, whose participation continually decreased. In some cases, the whites talked primarily to each other, shouting over the blacks.

This study has particular importance to bilingual and foreign language programs aimed at promoting positive interaction among members of different ethnic groups. Members of different ethnic groups may differ in their internalized status evaluations of self and others. Therefore, the most important consideration becomes, how can one intervene on status evaluations? A treatment program was designed to intervene on the process of status generalization. Black subjects were taught a new task: how to build a transistor radio. Care was taken to insure that they mastered the task, and were given feedback as to their mastery. Then, the black subjects taught white subjects of the same age to build the transistor, i.e., the white subjects were put into the situation of having to learn from the black students' superior knowledge. The session in which a black student taught white students was videotaped. Then, prior to playing "Kill the Bull," three treatments were applied to players. In Treatment A, only black expectations were treated: that is, the whites were not the students of the blacks; they arrived just in time to play the game. However, the black players were those who had learned to build the radio and teach the task to staff members, and they had been shown a videotape of their success doing the task and were therefore reinforced. In the other two treatments, both whites and blacks viewed a film of two competent black students building a radio, and of white students being taught to build a radio by a black student. After the treatments, all groups played the game. Analyses of the results have particular implications for bilingual education:

The most impressive and important finding is the need to treat both black and white expectations to attain equal status interaction in the integrated group. The failure of Treatment A to modify the white dominance pattern is most instructive, because it used the most often recommended method of increasing the self-confidence of people low in self-esteem. Treatment A used two major success experiences and much reinforcement from older, high status role models. The experience is analogous to recommending compensatory education for minority groups who do poorly in school (Cohen and Roper, p. 656).

Clearly, just treating the expectations of the low status individual or building up the self confidence of minorities alone will not cause effective interaction. Again, changing expectations to promote positive interaction among members of different cultures is a two-way process, requiring treatment for all parties involved. In the context of bilingual education, this means treating mainstream participants as well as minorities. The above example shows how treatments may be developed to intervene in the tendency to interpret new information on the basis of one's established frame of reference, which, in this case, includes a low status evaluation.

"Halo" versus "forked-tail" effect

People have a tendency to perceive others in terms of overall goodness or badness. The halo effect refers to perceiving people in terms of overall good—i.e., the person who can do no wrong. The forked-tail effect refers to the unfortunate person who can do nothing right.

In one study American subjects were shown pictures of people who differed in attractiveness. Then subjects were asked to judge others on a number of characteristics, including social desirability of personality, occupational status, marital competence, parental competence, and likelihood of marriage. Positive judgments in all dimensions corresponded to the degree of attractiveness perceived (Berscheid et al., 1971).

One can readily see how the halo effect might be influenced or even reversed by different cultural experiences. If the same study were to be conducted, using the same pictures, with members of a culture whose cues of physical attractiveness differed from those of Americans, judgments in relation to the pictures would probably differ markedly. Consider the implications for a person who is considered attractive in his/her own culture and thus tends to be positively evaluated on a variety of dimensions in interacting with other cultural members. Let us imagine the person is a black or Mexican-American student who is considered to be attractive within his/her own cultural group. The student is bussed across town to an all white suburb where the cues for attractiveness differ and the newcomer is perceived as unattractive. According to the forked-tail effect, the newcomer who was accustomed to receiving positive evaluations, might be evaluated negatively on a variety of dimensions. In such a circumstance, a variety of responses might occur. The white students who evaluated the black student negatively on first impression might hesitate or fail to interact with the newcomer. The newcomer, who was accustomed to positive evaluations might become quite baffled by the unfriendly treatment. As a result, the newcomer might seek increased interaction and affiliation among his/her own cultural group, thus tightening in-group/out-group distinctions rather than promoting positive interaction between the newcomers and the local residents.

Cue salience

Another cognitive bias which contributes to negative perceptions among people from different racial, ethnic and linguistic groups derives from the availability of particular cues in memory. Cues which are salient or distinctive appear to be remembered and retrieved from memory with greater frequency than common cues. For example, students may meet fifteen members of a given ethnic group who behave similarly to themselves and one who behaves differently. The one who is perceived as different will be the most available in memory. People also misjudge the frequency with which distinctive events occur, attributing more frequency to such events than occurs in reality (cf. Kahneman and Tversky, 1973). The Sydney study involving student impressions of people from foreign countries appeared to support this idea. As mentioned earlier, one frequent comment about the Italians was, "They're always wearing black." Members of the target culture who wore black clothing would be more salient and hence more remembered than those wearing multicolored clothing, which was similar to that of the Australian students. According to the notion of "misjudged frequency" of salient events, the number of people who wore black would be inflated, giving rise to the exaggerated "always." Familiarity and perceived similarity increases positive affiliation. By implication, perception of differences as opposed to the commonalities may, in turn, decrease positive affiliation and contribute toward negative evaluations.

Negative evaluations which are related to distinctive features tend to be more available in memory; therefore these impressions are more lasting and harder to change than positive ones. This notion has been termed the "negative effect" and has been widely reported in the psychological literature (cf. Hodges, 1974; Hamilton and Zanna, 1972; and Warr, 1974).

Although people average available traits to arrive at a complete impression, they weigh negative information more heavily than they do positive information (Hodges, 1974).

The negative effect may also be related to a cost-orientation notion.

The idea is that people are more concerned with costs than benefits when they make a decision. As a result, they scan the alternatives more carefully for their defects than for their assets, and take possible defects more seriously in making their decision (Freedman *et al.*).

One could argue that the relevance of the cost-orientation explanation might differ across cultures. Assets may be more salient in some cultures than costs. The variance would be analogical to a teacher who critiques a paper for what is lacking contrasted with the teacher who critiques the same paper for what it contributes. A series of ethnographic interviews with a student from India at Stanford (reported in the Appendix to this book) suggested that the cost-orientation explanation is more representative of American society than Indian society. The student felt that Americans were always trying to dissect and poke holes in ideas rather than seeing their overall merit. If cost-orientation does contribute to the negative effect, and this orientation is influenced by culture, then people from cost-oriented cultures such as the United States might underestimate the benefits people from different cultures contribute, and overestimate their costs.

To summarize, characteristics that are uncommon to the perceiver are often the most distinctive. Therefore, perceptions of people from different cultures may reflect the differences, even though these differences may not be the most representative of the person or group. To counteract the negative effect, bilingual, second language and foreign language instruction aimed at developing positive perceptions among people from different cultures might intentionally focus on similarities which often go unnoticed. (As we saw in an earlier section of this chapter, similarity in its own right influences liking.) While this may appear trivial, it is not trivial in the context of what is being taught in bilingual, foreign language and ethnic studies programs. Typically, the target culture is introduced through a description of unique characteristics—that which distinguishes the target culture of study from other cultures. In other words, cultural courses generally begin with dissimilarities. As we have seen, perception of dissimilarities over similarities is quite a normal tendency; however, it constitutes a cognitive bias. (As I mentioned in Chapter 1, in Papua New Guinea I even caught myself taking pictures of the exotic tribesmen wearing leaves rather than the boys wearing jeans, who were equally common and equally authentic!)

To counter this normal tendency I have asked foreign students in several ESL courses to focus on similarities. In a program at Stanford University, I simply said, "Similarities bring people together; differences often separate, so your assignment is to go out and look for similarities. Walk around campus, go into coffee shops, talk to people, observe and listen. Everywhere you go for the next two days, actively look for similarities." One student responded as follows:

I have noticed several things in common with American people. My friends and I went to a pizza house tonight and talked about marriage with an American student. He said that some American women are satisfied with housekeeping, and others are not. The same thing can be said about Japanese women. Today, more women have jobs in both America and Japan. They have their own opinion and identity. Such a change in women's attitudes can be seen in both countries. The other thing I have noticed was that American students enjoy freedom here as we do. We came to an American university for the first time, and we have got freedom. My friend said that American students also felt they had freedom when they came here. They also stay outdoors late at night as we do.

I thought American people had much more freedom than we did, but I realized they had the same feelings as ours. I found students in both countries have something in common and I felt happy to realize that.

Students at the Center for Language and Crosscultural Skills were asked to explain what similarities they discovered between themselves and Americans during Center activities. The following is one student's response.

In "New Games Day" we played with Americans. In play, we don't need language. We smile, laugh at each other, hold hands together, and it was enough to communicate our own feelings. I could feel that I was feeling the same way as the people who were there, inspite of Japanese or Americans. I could feel we were sharing the same feeling. At that day, for the first time, I could think that there is no difference between Americans and me.

ESL teachers could focus on similarities even through the most structured linguistic exercises, such as sentence completion:

(*Another student*) is similar to me in that (*he/she*) (*verb*)

Bilingual, second language and foreign language instruction might also deliberately emphasize the benefits people from different cultures contribute. Bilingual instruction might be organized to insure that members of different cultures provide essential assets from the point of view of mainstream students, so that benefits of mutual interaction outweigh the costs. The radio training treatment for intervening in status generalization provides a concrete example.

Faulty inferences and attribution errors

Person perception often involves making inferences. The study of how people make inferences about others is referred to as "attribution theory." Observers attribute causality to overt behavior by making inferences about non-observed states. For example, "John is talking fast; therefore he is nervous or angry."

People do not always draw accurate inferences about other people, especially where people from cultures different from their own are concerned. Sometimes faulty inferences are the result of inaccurate or incomplete information, as we saw in the analysis of how communication breaks down. To the extent that the meaning associated with the same cue differs across cultures and the target cultural meaning is unknown, faulty inferences may result. These types of errors may be corrected with information; educators can develop exercises which focus on the production of correct inferences related to target cultural stimuli, (provided the information does not produce dissonance). One study showed that the production of inferences could be improved through exercises designed to focus on the inferences children make in relation to pictures (Higgins, 1931). More difficult to correct are faulty inferences which result from cognitive biases involving salience of particular cues, and errors in attributing causality, referred to as "attribution errors."

Salience and causality: "seeing is believing"

Salient cues are also perceived as the most *causally influential*. These cues are the most available in memory. Whatever is perceptually salient will attract the dominant causal explanation. For example:

The man who is running down the street is seen as causing the bank's alarm system to go off. (Taylor and Fiske, 1975).

Analogously, if two men were running down the street and one was black, the other white, a white observer might tend to attribute causality to the black. Similarly, let us suppose a conversation takes place among three people, one of whom has a foreign accent. The conversation ends in disagreement. The person who spoke with the foreign accent might be perceived as the more influential in causing the disagreement. However, salience might also result in overestimating the positive contribution of the most salient person. In one experiment, three group discussions were arranged: in one, all participants were white. Another included one black. In the third, participants were evenly divided in race.

The same tape recording was used in all cases, but each speaker was identified with a still slide as he spoke, and the race of the speakers was varied. Subjects who were exposed to this mixed-media discussion rated the speakers for amount of contribution to the discussion. The "solo" black stood out as talking more, being more influential, and giving a clearer impression than did the same speaker in either of the other contexts, where his race did not make him so salient (Taylor *et al.*, 1977).

This relationship between salience and attribution of causality can be put to positive use in classes. Members of the target culture in foreign language classes may be soloed among members of the learners' culture while the group is engaged in positive behaviors. Children of linguistic and ethnic minorities may play a similar role in culturally mixed classrooms.

Judging ourselves versus others

Psychologically speaking, we are more charitable about excusing our own behavior than that of others. If we have a problem, "it's the circumstances." But if we see a problem occurring with someone else, it is likely to be "their fault," their personality, etc. Observers make a fundamental attribution error in judging the causes of other peoples' behavior. They tend to overestimate the importance of other people's dispositions and underestimate the external factors related to the situation. Conversely, people tend to overestimate the external factors related to their own behavior and underestimate the internal or dispositional factors. That is, the acts of other people reflect their attitudes, dispositions, internal motivations, but our own acts reflect the context we are in. This judgmental error may be due to the salience of other people's behavior, which tends to dominate our perceptual field. We can see another person's actual behavior, which then becomes more salient than the other person's situation. Conversely, we cannot see our own behaviour; instead, factors in the situation or environment are more salient. A student visiting a foreign country, who has difficulty making friends with the local people, may explain the situation in terms of language differences, differences in customs, or unfriendly behaviors on the part of the people, rather than in terms of his own personality or inadequacy of interpersonal skills. Conversely, the same student might judge the behavior of an immigrant in terms of the immigrant's personality, or attitudes. A person who felt uncomfortable with a Latin American's body language or spatial proximity in a conversation might attribute the other person's behavior to his/her pushiness rather than to differences in customs and speech conventions. Numerous psychological studies support the attribution error (cf. Heider, 1958; Jones and Nisbett, 1972; Snyder and Jones, 1974). Attribution of causality to another person's disposition appears particularly strong when an observer sees or hears another person. This finding may have important implications for the use of films to present members of the target culture. Often students in foreign language classes and other programs concerned with teaching culture are familiarized with the target culture through films, which are generally used as supplementary activities, presented without detailed explanations of the factors which make up the context of the situation and are not integrated into instructional units. Such use of films may increase the attribution error, since students may over-attribute causality of events to the disposition of the people observed. Disposition, in turn, is evaluated on the basis of behavior. As we have seen in previous sections, target cultural behaviour may well be misinterpreted owing to mismatches in cues and schema. Without intervention, faulty inferences and crosscultural misunderstandings may be promoted.

Many foreign language textbooks introduce the target culture through short cultural notes in texts. As with films, these notes generally are not integrated into the instructional units. Due possibly to their brevity, they frequently focus on descriptions of cultural events or culturally appropriate behaviors in particular situation. As with films, these short notes may promote rather than intervene in attribution errors. In order to intervene in attribution errors, textbook writers and teachers may want to focus on background, situational features. When using films, teachers may want to focus on the context of events, de-emphasizing the behaviors in the foreground. Students will need to learn the cultural background for the behavior itself, that is, the function of the behavior and the rules underlying the behavior. In this regard, the functional approach to culture, defined in Chapter 2, may be very helpful. Films and notes which are integrated within instructional units develop a deeper understanding of these underlying rules and functions, and the particular cues and schema that are operating within the target culture.

Intervening in attribution errors through empathy and analogy

Development of empathy through direct experience or analogy are useful techniques to counter attribution errors. During five experiments, subjects heard speakers present speeches written by students who were assigned to advocate a particular position. Subjects were *told* that the speaker was only reading a speech on behalf of someone else; the speaker was deliberately unenthusiastic. However, the subjects perceived the position expressed in the speech as the *true* position of the speaker. In order to intervene in the attribution error, a subsequent experiment was conducted in which the subjects themselves were instructed to write an essay advocating both positions that were reflected in the speeches they were going to hear. After *experiencing* the fact than an essay writer or speaker might not have a choice about the position taken, students did not perceive the speaker's position as his true position (Snyder and Jones, 1974). In another study, observers were instructed to empathize with the actor:

Please try to empathize with the girl on the left side of the screen. *Imagine how Margaret feels* as she engages in the conversation. While you are watching the tape, *picture to yourself* just how she feels in the situation (Regan and Totten, 1975).

Observers who empathized with the actors and viewed them more from their own perspective also judged the actors' actions more similarly to their own. That is, the observers attributed actors' behavior more to their situation than to their dispositions.

The studies reported here have important implications for intervening in attribution errors which students in bilingual, second language and foreign language programs may make about members of different cultures. Exercises could be developed in which students empathize with the target cultural member. For example, target cultural events could be presented to students through written and visual materials, followed by exercises in which students were instructed to think of analogous situations in their own lives. First, students could describe how they would act in an analogous situation which was relevant to their own lives and then explain why they would behave in such a way, and how they would feel. The following excerpt is taken from an interview between an Australian teacher and Italian child. The excerpt provides an example of materials that could be used for developing empathy through analogy:

Mario is 14—Sicilian—his hand is on his plump chest. "They call me a fat wop, miss. I know I'm fat—but my mum, she cries if I don't eat everything she gives me. 'I've been cooking for you all day, son,' she says. 'Don't you want what I make you?' So I eat. It's bad enough being fat—but maybe one day when I'm older, I can fix that. But being a wop—well, ya can't stop being Italian, can you?" (Brotherhood of St. Lawrence, 1971).

Students could be asked to imagine the boy's feelings and how they would feel. Students could also be asked if they have ever been in a similar or analogous situation: "Have you ever been criticized for something you felt you could not change? How did you feel?"

TESOL Certificate students in crosscultural communication at the University of California, Berkeley, were asked to develop strategies for promoting empathy and the perception of similarity through analogy. One group devised a series of exercises beginning with the story of a newly arrived student who came from Vietnam. One exercise instructed students to write their own short story about a situation which was new to them and which made them a little afraid because they did not know what to expect. In another exercise, called the "newcomer game," all students (newcomers and mainstream alike) were instructed to complete the following sentences orally:

I felt embarrassed when ____.
I felt lonely when ____.
I felt confused when ____.
I felt frightened when I first ____.

By developing empathy with members of the target culture, students should become more accustomed to seeing situational causes of their behavior as well as dispositional ones.

Summary

In summary, experience within a culture influences how we perceive other people. People use cues and schemas through which to anticipate and interpret the behavior of others. Each of these is related to cultural experience. *Positive perceptions* of other people are related to *perceptual matches* between what is anticipated and what is perceived, the *positivity* of traits perceived and the extent of *similarity perceived*. Conversely *negative perceptions* and *crosscultural misunderstandings* are related to perceptual *mismatches* and *differences perceived*. Our internal director interprets the movie differently. Scripts do not match; cues do not match; values do not match. Many mismatches are the result of unexpected, actual differences in the behavior of people from other cultures: different cultural assumptions about situations, different ways of structuring information, different ways of speaking and different ways of interacting in terms of reciprocal and non-reciprocal speech. Misunderstandings of this type may be avoided or remedied by knowledge and skills. However, information about the target culture may not be sufficient to remedy misunderstandings, once negative impressions are formed. While differences may be causing the problem, explicit focus on the differences will not always help; it may even hinder in the case of cognitive biases.

People are not always rational. We often do not perceive things as they actually are. Certain cognitive biases are quite normal. We make first impressions based on limited experience and information. We have a tendency for consistency; this encourages us to interpret new information selectively to fit these impressions, and to discount what does not fit. We misjudge the frequency and importance of salient events. We make errors in judging causality. Judging other people as we judge ourselves is particularly difficult.

None of the above cognitive biases are inherently negative. They are normal tendencies of human information processing. We can use what we know to good advantage. But any effective programs aimed at developing affiliation and interaction with people from different cultures must involve all parties concerned in the interaction—the L1 and L2 speaker, the mainstream and the minority alike.

The following is a checklist of implications for ESL, FL and bilingual programs:

1. Provide knowledge of target cultural cues, schemas, meaning systems, and the correct inferences that may be drawn from particular cues.
2. Insure that a positive first impression is made.
3. Focus on similarities.
4. Counter negative evaluations such as low status, powerlessness, exclusion, by making each student's skills/participation necessary for others.
5. Lessen attribution errors by focusing on background and situational factors underlying behaviors, and have learners emphathize with members of the target culture by making analogies to their own experience and through the stimulation of feelings.
6. People project their feelings of self onto the evaluation of others. Avoid embarrassment in the second and foreign language classrooms, threat by mainstream students in bilingual classrooms, and powerlessness of bilingual students in classrooms.
7. Treat all parties involved in interaction—not just cultural or language minorities.

Although we may not be the rational animals we have considered ourselves to be, we can use the same principles that cause misunderstandings and negative perceptions to create positive perceptions and affiliations with people from different cultures.

Chapter 6

How can we facilitate positive impressions of people from other cultures? The role of ethnography

We may conclude from the last chapter that an ideal approach to crosscultural understanding promotes positive impressions among people of different cultures from the beginning. The anthropological method, "ethnography," may be particularly useful in developing such positive impressions. As a descriptive technique, ethnography is useful in obtaining cultural information and evaluating instruction. As a process, doing ethnography facilitates interaction and deeper understanding among people from the different cultures involved. The ethnography included in the Appendix, "How does it feel to be a graduate student from India at Stanford?" illustrates each of these uses.

What is ethnography?

In the most simple terms, ethnography is a method of describing a culture or situation within a culture from the "emic" or native's point of view, i.e., from the point of view of the cultural actor.

This approach to ethnography seeks to describe a culture in its own terms. The aim of ethnographic semantics is to discover the characteristic ways a people categorize, code and define their own experience (Spradley and McCurdy, 1972, p. viii).

Frequently ethnography employs a variety of techniques, including interviews and participant-observations. Ethnography is different from other observational techniques in that it does not pre-structure or precategorize what is to be observed, it elicits observer participation and interpretation, and it takes place in a non-laboratory setting.

Categorizing experience

The purpose of ethnography is to find out the way people within the target culture categorize and prioritize experience. Ethnography does not apply concepts for crosscultural comparisons, i.e., "etic" concepts, before such concepts naturally emerge as part of the culture being described. For example, an ethnographer would not ask, "Who is your best friend?" before the category, friends and the idea of hierarchy among friends emerged naturally as relevant to the particular culture or situation being described. The ethnographic method aims to decrease bias by not pre-selecting what is observed on the basis of the observer's predefined cultural categories. Of course the ethnographer, like any observer, does filter information through predefined categories to a certain extent. As we saw in Chapters 3 and 5, people filter and interpret all new experience through past experience. However, the ethnographic approach does lead to more open observations because it does not contain predefined questionnaires or categories.

Observer as participant

Ethnographers not only observe, but also participate. The more ethnographers get "inside the picture," the more accurately they are able to describe the way insiders feel, the competencies they acquire to behave appropriately and the way they anticipate and interpret events. I am reminded of one anthropologist's ethnographic account of how one becomes a Buddhist monk. He became one! That is, he developed the competencies one needs to function as a monk, to interact with others as a monk, to anticipate events as a monk, and to structure and experience *his* day as a monk (Textor, 1978b).

Some criticize that the participant-observer role increases subjectivity of reporting. However, to the extent that the ethnographer loses objectivity and interprets things from the native's point of view, we are getting an inside, emic account of culture.

Believing ... that man is an animal suspended in webs of significance he himself has spun, I take culture to be those webs, and the analysis of it to be therefore not an experimental science in search of law, but an interpretive one in search of meaning (Geertz, 1973, p. 5).

From another perspective, education itself is a subjective, value-laden process, notwithstanding the frequent emphasis on objectivity.

Education is a normative enterprise, and I believe that much too much social science attempts to be value-neutral in order to increase scientific objectivity. This aspiration, of course, is hopeless. Scientific work in any field is never value-neutral. Social scientists select the problems they will inquire into; in this selection, values are at work. Social scientists choose the methods they will use; in this choice, values are expressed. Social scientists interpret the data they secure; here too, values are employed. Social scientists assign significance to their findings; to do this requires one to make value judgments. ... To claim that science is value saturated is not to complain but rather to give scientific inquiry its due. Its negation is what is worth complaining about (Eisner, 1979).

While interpretation on the part of ethnographers is critical, they have an obligation to indicate *when* they are interpreting and *why*. Thorough explanations will include the experience ethnographers bring to the situation as well as the particular behavior(s) or event(s) in the target cultural situation that lead them to that conclusion.

Non-laboratory setting

Ethnography does not take place in a laboratory, with experimentals and controls. Reporting is often in the form of a case study rather than in measurable, quantifiable data.

To be taken seriously, to be viable, and to be relevant, social science must dare to study the real problems of men and society, must use the real community, the market place, the arena of politics and power as its laboratories, and must confront and seek to understand the dynamics of social action and social change (Pelto, 1970, p. 321).

Educational researchers and social scientists have often confused what is knowable, learnable and describable from what is quantifiable and measurable. As pointed out in Chapter 2, too much emphasis may be placed on what is verifiable, to the detriment of cultural understanding. The insistence upon measurable procedures may result in a narrow range of facts and interpretations. In contrast, ethnographers provide in-depth case studies of particular cultural situations, full of rich description. Their accounts are more similar to literary descriptions than to scientific reports.

Obtaining cultural information for the content of instruction

Ethnography is a useful method to obtain cultural information about the target culture for incorporation into the content of instruction. Often the cultural content of foreign language, second language, and bilingual programs reflects a limited, if not inaccurate account of the target culture. For example, teaching aspects of the target culture in these programs often reflects non-native accounts of "the family, foods, leisure." The accounts are often based on observable aspects of behaviors and customs, or on categories pre-set by the researcher/writer. As we learned in Chapters 3 and 5, many crosscultural problems may not be attributable to observable differences, but rather to the way we categorize, interpret and evaluate events.

To describe a culture is not to recount the events of a society but to specify what one must know to make those events maximally probable. . . . The test of descriptive adequacy must always refer to informants' interpretations of events, not simply to the occurrence of events (Frake, 1962).

We do not have many, if any, good ethnographies of the cultures corresponding to the languages most commonly taught in American schools and universities. For example, we do not have many adequate accounts of the French family or the Mexican family to incorporate into French, Spanish or bilingual courses. More importantly, we do not know the emic categories and definitions through which French or Mexican people interpret the world, individually, or as a group. We have more ethnographies of exotic cultures than of the cultures corresponding to the most commonly taught languages. By doing ethnographies of the cultures relevant to local societies and providing authentic accounts, ethnography can contribute an essential first step in culture teaching: namely, what to teach.

Obtaining cultural information for use in methodology

Ethnography is also a valuable tool for obtaining cultural information on *how* to teach, e.g., how to organize instruction so as to implement cultural diversity and transmit cultural goals. For example, Chapter 3 discussed how different cultures have different preferred modes of presenting and responding to information. It was suggested that effective methodologies in bilingual, second language and foreign language programs build a bridge between the home and school cultures. Elsewhere I have referred to this idea as a "cultural merger" in the methodology, which must also take place if a student from one culture is to effectively understand a second language and culture (Robinson, 1981).

The United States Civil Rights Commission Report, 1973, disclosed that Mexican-American students received unequal treatment in schooling. Similarly, in the case of Lau versus Nichols, the United States Supreme Court decided that Lau, a Chinese student, was denied equality of educational opportunity because education was not responsive to his cultural and linguistic needs. As a result, schools have a mandate to be "culturally responsive" (U.S. Dept. of Health, Education and Welfare, 1975).

Before education in multicultural societies can be equitable and culturally responsive, before second and foreign language classes can implement cultural mergers in methodology, we need to obtain information regarding how teaching and learning experiences are organized and interpreted in the cultures represented in our society and schools; e.g., how do students and teachers interact with each other, and what events are anticipated in particular cultural situations?

Ethnography can make an essential contribution to cultural knowledge in this area. Through the role of participant-observer, the ethnographer develops and describes the competencies necessary to function within a culture.

We have tended to think of description as simply a matter of presenting the "objective" facts about a society, its organization, laws, customs and shared beliefs. We have not been seriously concerned, until very recently, to know how to behave acceptably (within the target society) . . . We have wanted to know *about* other societies, not how to be competent in the things their members are expected to be competent in (Erickson *et al.*, 1978).

In providing culturally responsive education, knowledge of these competencies is critical. Bilingual and second language instruction will be more effective if educators know *how* to effectively communicate with culturally diverse learners, how to recognize different expressions of attention or desire to respond, how to implement different means of conveying praise or criticism, and how to anticipate and interpret culturally different behaviors.

Several ethnographies aimed at identifying such competencies have recently emerged, (cf. Spindler, 1982). One study addressed questions such as the following:

1. In bilingual first grade classrooms, are there different sets of cultural rules of social appropriateness or etiquette in communication which are analytically distinguishable as *Latino* and *Anglo* interactional styles, respectively?
2. Do children and teachers who vary in knowledge of language structure also vary in knowledge of *communicative function*; i.e., in the uses of communicative behavior, verbal and nonverbal, for social purposes in classroom interaction?

   Do teachers and children who are bilingual use *Latino cultural etiquette* when speaking Spanish? (If so, how, how often and in what circumstances?)

   Do these teachers and children use *Latino cultural etiquette* when speaking English? (Erickson *et al.*, 1978, p. 8).

There is already some evidence which suggests that teachers who speak the same language, e.g., English, but have diverse cultural backgrounds, e.g. Latino, Anglo, Native American, have developed different ways of praising and sanctioning students (Philips, 1972, Erickson and Mohatt, 1977, Erickson *et al.*, 1978).

Latino Teacher *Example*: "Private Praise'
During a reading lesson, the teacher is making his/her rounds in the classroom while the students are busily engaged in some reading exercise task. As the teacher approaches Juan's desk, Juan, a Spanish dominant bilingual, tells the teacher that he has finished the task. Reviewing the paper, the teacher gently smiles while simultaneously touching Juan's shoulder and slightly nodding his/her head in a positive manner (up and down).

Anglo Teacher *Example*: "Public Praise"
In an analogous event (reading) as the Latino teacher above, Johnny informs the teacher that he has finished the assigned task. Reviewing the paper, the teacher states in a somewhat loud and enthusiastic manner (so the entire class can hear), "Very good, Johnny, Nice work!" (Erickson *et al.*, 1978, p. 3).

Cultural knowledge, such as the above Latino pattern of praising, often goes unnoticed in traditional observational instruments such as the Flanders system of classroom interaction analysis. Categories in the latter tend to be pre-set according to a traditionally Anglo form of reinforcement, namely public, verbal questioning, reprimanding and praise. Ethnographic research identifies cultural information which can contribute to culturally responsive teaching strategies and cultural mergers between the learner's home culture and target culture of study. However, such information can only be obtained through in-depth, well-developed ethnographic studies which provide readers with extensive background data regarding the characteristics of the particular people and situation(s) investigated. Care must be taken to avoid overgeneralizing and stereotyping on the basis of a few, brief ethnographic observations that lack sufficient background data.

Evaluating fulfillment of cultural goals

Once we have identified relevant cultural information to incorporate into course content and methodology, ethnography may also be used as a method of evaluating the extent to which this information and related cultural goals are reflected in classroom practices. Other methods of evaluating cultural goals frequently employ predominantly quantitative, psychological techniques such as attitude questionnaires, semantic differentials and ethnocentrism scales. Fulfillment of cultural goals may be deduced, somewhat indirectly. Through ethnographic interviews, participant-observations and qualitative descriptions, ethnography may be used to directly evaluate cultural goals, i.e., are we practicing what we are preaching? For example, do teacher-student and student-student interactions in bilingual classrooms reflect the cultural diversity intended? In second and foreign language classrooms, do these interactions reflect both the home and target cultural styles? In multicultural classrooms, do students of different cultural backgrounds have equal status, and do they participate equally in leadership activities? Do foreign language students exhibit positive attitudes and behaviors toward speakers of the target language? Combination of ethnographic interviews, participant-observations and detailed descriptions give multiple perspectives through which to answer these questions. The use of ethnography is not in conflict with other research methods. Indeed, the use of ethnographic techniques in conjunction with quantitative methods may lead to powerful, generalizable findings.

Do students in multicultural classrooms participate equally?

The status intervention study cited in Chapter 5 combined ethnographic techniques with video analysis to evaluate the extent of equal participation among black and white students who played the game, "Kill the Bull." Through intensive observation and micro-analysis of videotaped segments, the researchers found that the black students' attempt to speak and participate in the solution was not recognized by the white students, who shouted them down, spoke to each other, and took control of the decision-making process. After the intervention program took place, the game was again played and videotaped so the effects of the treatment could be evaluated. The analysis showed an increase in the recognition of the black students' attempt to participate and an increase in actual participation in the decision-making process (Cohen and Roper, 1972). This research is an example of how intensive observational techniques may be used to directly identify whether the goals of cultural equality and respect for cultural diversity are being fulfilled. Rosenfeld's ethnography of a Harlem School and McDermott's account of how black pariah children achieve school failure provide other examples of how ethnographic, qualitative methods serve as a critical point of departure in identifying specific practices that reflect cultural inequality versus cultural responsiveness (Rosenfeld, 1971; McDermott, 1974).

Do teachers and students perceive other students the same way?

Teacher perceptions of what is going on in the classroom may not coincide with student perceptions. Through ethnographic observations, as well as interviews with teachers and students, Spindler (1974) found large discrepancies between teacher and student perceptions of the behavior and status of particular students. In the case study of Beth Anne, a middle class white student, interviews with teachers disclosed the following:

The teachers all expressed verbal agreement that Beth Anne was indeed very well adjusted, both academically and socially (Spindler, 1974, p. 141).

Ethnographic observations conflicted with teacher opinion:

She interacted only infrequently with other children in the classroom either in the room or on the playground.... She played organized games but not enthusiastically and seemed to find aggressive handling of a ball or other play equipment difficult (*Ibid.*).

When students were asked, "Whom would you like to sit next to?" and were administered a status-reputation test, the following results occurred:

The results from both techniques indicate that Beth Anne is marginal in the classroom group. She is given very little attention—either favorable or unfavorable. It is almost as though she were not there at all (*Ibid.*, p. 145).

Spindler suggests that the case of Beth Anne demonstrates how culturally unsophisticated teacher perceptions may damage the successful middle-class child as well as the academically unsuccessful minority child in the school.

Most teachers are idealistic, many are quite liberal in their political and social beliefs, but they are products of their culture and live within the framework of values and symbols that are a part of that culture. By being made aware of what they are and do, they can be freed from the tyranny of their cultures; in turn, they will be able to free children from the damaging effects of premature, inaccurate, or prejudiced estimates and interpretations of their behavior that are culturally induced (*Ibid.*, p. 152).

Does language fluency mean a foreign-language student has a positive attitude toward members of the target culture?

Foreign language educators have long claimed that study of a foreign language leads to a positive understanding of those who speak the language. Elsewhere I have suggested that this may constitute "a magic-carpet ride to another culture syndrome!" (Robinson, 1978b). Ethnography may be useful in evaluating this claim (or syndrome).

I used ethnographic techniques, including participant-observations, interviews and qualitative description to evaluate a Spanish program at Stanford university for one week. During the daily review and interpretation of my notes, I began to realize how my own background as a language student, a language researcher, and a university language teacher was influencing my reporting. I began wondering how students really did feel about Spanish, so I interviewed one student after class that day. The following is an excerpt from the report that resulted. The use of first person and subjective interpretations may appear contrary to traditional academic reporting. As mentioned earlier, interpretation is a primary task of ethnography; however, ethnographers are obliged to describe their own background, when they are interpreting, and why they are making the particular interpretations in question. Use of the first person helps to communicate this intentional personalism of interpretation and inhibits communication of unintended generalizations.

I chose this particular student because I thought he was the "best" student in the class ... the most attentive, the most fluent, answered quickly, answered correctly, answered with a good accent, watched the teacher during every question, looked at each student during every response and was usually sitting up and smiling. I chose "the best" student because I wanted a positive point of view. Too often we knock things down. I felt I had been doing that in my own notes, so I wanted a different perspective. Since I considered him to be such a good student, I naturally assumed that he must be interested in some aspect of the Spanish speaking world and probably had Spanish-speaking friends. I wanted to see to what extent my perceptions of his matched his own point of view, so I approached him after class. ... Here is what resulted. (I = interviewer/self; S = student).

I: What made you take Spanish?
S: I'm a graduating senior. I wanted an easy course. It's easy.
I: Is there any other reason you took it?
S: I like languages. I'm good at them.
I: Then why did you start this late?
S: I doubt I'll have to use it. I'm one of the pragmatic students. Even though I'm good at languages, there's not much use for Spanish—not in everyday life, even though it did help when I was working in a bank.
I: How much time do you spend on homework?
S: About two hours a week ... but before a mid-term, about four hours.
I: I noticed you seemed pretty attentive. Are you interested in Spanish?
S: Yes. I'm attentive in all my classes. If someone's doing a performance, I think students ought to pay attention. Besides, I've had to work to put myself through school, and when you're paying for it, you pay attention.
I: You said you were good at languages, and I noticed you have a very good accent in Spanish. Why do you think that is?
S: Well I used to live in Texas. I went to a Catholic school.
I: Were there any Spanish speakers there?
S: I said I went to a Catholic school in Texas didn't I?
I: I guess there were many Mexican-Americans.

S: Sure.

I: Were they bilingual?

S: Yes.

I: Did you ever speak Spanish with them?

S: Just to tell dirty jokes.

I: Why?

S: They sound so much dirtier in Spanish . . . you can roll those "r"s . . . you can use your hands!

I: Well, you have a good accent.

S: My grandfather speaks Spanish (then the student added quickly) but not naturally. He had a lot of wetbacks working for him. He would just say, "I want you to plant the seeds over there . . . I want you to pick that". . . . He was good at giving orders in Spanish.

I: Did you take Spanish in high school?

S: No, I took French.

I: You had such a good start in Spanish. Why did you take French?

S: It sounded neater than Spanish.

I: Did you make any Spanish-speaking friends in high school?

S: Not really. I stuck with the whites. In high school we moved to central California and everything was pretty racist there.

I: Who do you mean by "non-whites"?

S: Oh, the blacks, the hispanics . . . but Señora Sanchez and people like here . . . she's white. (Sra. Sanchez was his teacher, who was born in Spain.)

I: So none of your close friends are non-whites?

S: Not really.

I: How do you feel about this Spanish course?

S: I like it.

I: How would you rank it against your other courses?

S: Well, I have five courses. I guess I'd put Spanish second from the top.

I: Has this course made you want to visit any Spanish-speaking countries?

S: Not really. I mean, I've always known that I'll go to Europe. I wouldn't mind sitting on the beach in Spain drinking sangria.

Well, all I can say is things aren't always what they seem! Immediately after the interview I thought that my perceptions couldn't have been more inaccurate; everything seemed so opposite. Then I realized that my observations were not inaccurate; only my *interpretations* of them were. I had observed that this student was attentive, and he was; that he liked Spanish, and he did; that he had a good accent, and he had. I interpreted these observations to mean that he wanted to talk to Spanish-speaking people. His lack of perceived "use" of Spanish, in a country where Spanish is so widely spoken, was somehow less surprising (I guess I really mean less objectionable to me) than his disinterest, if not negative, colonialist attitude toward some Spanish-speaking peoples. But then, I had my multi-colored glasses on and I was interpreting in terms of *my own* reasons for studying Spanish. . . .

To repeat the obvious, what appears to be, on the basis of observations or language fluency *per se*, is insufficient in determining fulfillment of cultural goals. The combination of a variety of techniques including ethnographic interviews with teachers and students, participant-observations, qualitative descriptions and quantitative findings will yield more effective evaluations.

Ethnography as a process which promotes understanding and positive interactions

We have seen how ethnography may be used to obtain cultural information and to evaluate whether the information and related cultural goals are reflected in the practices and attitudes of teachers and students. The process of doing ethnography may promote understanding and positive interactions between members of different cultural groups. The process, in its own right, becomes a direct means of breaking down cultural barriers due to at least five factors, which are intrinsic to the ethnographic method: (1) the commitment of time on the part of both the ethnographer and informant(s); (2) the depth of discussion or observations related to a particular topic; (3) the need for creative listening; (4) the self-awareness of one's own communication style and one's own culture; and (5) the role of being a participant as well as an observer, and thereby sharing part of the target cultural experience.

Commitment of time

Simply stated, ethnographies take time, be it an ethnographic interview involving one key informant, the case study of a classroom or the ethnographic study of an entire culture. Both the ethnographer and informants agree to commit themselves to spending time with one another. As mentioned in Chapter 5, some psychological studies suggest that mere exposure and continued proximity to another person increase liking (Zajonc, 1968). The commitment to taking the time to get to know someone else has particular relevance for understanding and overcoming the differences between people of different cultures. One might ask oneself *when* one last took the time to understand a stranger, particularly one from another culture, whom one perceived as culturally different. With the competing demands of time in an industrial society such as the United States, if people take any time to know someone at all, it is most probably someone with whom they have a mutual affinity or perceive as similar. In the next chapter we will see that time is a critical condition in modifying negative perceptions of other people. Ethnography provides the setting for taking the time to know people whom we may otherwise fail to communicate with at all, or whom we approach with barriers and stereotypes.

Depth of discussion and observations

The ethnographer and informants take the time to go into depth. A characteristic of ethnographic interviews is to ask a general, grand tour question and follow it where it may lead, in depth. The ethnographer probes a particular category until it (or the informant) appears to be exhausted! This in-depth discussion is contrasted with interviews and discussions which are marked by frequent changes of topic, to keep the conversation moving.

In-depth discussions build deeper rapport between the speech partners. By definition, they are deeper, both cognitively and affectively. Going into depth often allows both partners to realize fundamental commonalities which are frequently blocked by initially perceived differences.

Creative listening

Conducting an ethnographic interview requires creative, active listening. Contrasted with an uninterested, polite conversationalist who asks a question and turns a deaf ear to the response, ethnographers express their interest and attention by asking questions related to the response. The ethnographer's interest and active listening contribute to the informant's positive attitude toward the ethnographer. Spradley and McCurdy noted that "the opportunity to talk for hours about their life style was gratifying to informants and resulted in numerous long-term friendships" among college students who were ethnographers and informants (Spradley and McCurdy, 1972).

I remember a story told by my first psychology professor. He was talking about how people respond to good listeners.

Have you ever been to a party . . . found someone you could talk to for hours, and you did . . . you kept on talking. . . . You come home, think about the evening and your new-found friend, and sum him up by saying, "Gee, he was a good conversationalist!"

Self-awareness: learning by contrast

Taking the time to listen to other people go into depth about their ideas, experiences and feelings is by no means a one-way experience. The process provides a remarkable experience of self-awareness: awareness of one's own ability to communicate and awareness of one's own culture. Ethnographic descriptions and definitions of particular cultural categories are often identified by the principle of contrast:

Category systems not only divide up the world, they also define it. In order to make sense out of human behaviour we must begin with the actor's definition of the situation, and a crucial feature of such meaning systems is the principle of contrast. The meaning of a concept cannot be made clear without specifying what it contrasts with. The principle of contrast suggests that what something *does mean* is intimately linked to what it *does not mean* (Spradley and McCurdey, 1972).

Ethnographers learn about their own culture and values by comparison and contrast with the informant's point of view. In using ethnography with college anthropology students, some researchers found that ethnography helped to reduce ethnocentrism.

The greatest single challenge in teaching undergraduates was to help them become aware of their own ethnocentrism as well as other people's cultural perspectives. But some research approaches did not accomplish this very well. For instance, a student could interview members of some cultural group during a semester without gaining this awareness. . . . So we began to experiment with those methods that most effectively changed the student's view of his own cultural values (*Ibid.*).

I asked graduate students of TESOL at the University of California, Berkeley, to conduct and report an ethnographic interview. One student interviewed Nhi, a female Vietnamese refugee, whom the student later learned was a physician in Saigon. The excerpt begins with the words of Nhi, followed by the student's comments:

"The real difficulties started for me after I was officially admitted and recognized as an American doctor.

First of all there was a language barrier. It took me two years to gain my actual knowledge of English, although I had gotten a certain English ability fifteen, twenty years ago. Communication is still in English something new for me as well as for most Vietnamese people." I asked her to elaborate on what she meant by communication. She responded, "Because of my inability to speak fluent English my financial situation is not so good. My financial problem has not allowed me to get to the hospitals in remote areas of the East Coast where I would have more opportunities than in California. It is painful for my people not to be able to better express their goals and desires with their lives. This will come slowly with time." At this point Nhi was in tears. We ended the conversation by promising to get together the next Friday. My feelings were those of compassion, frustration, anger, depression and powerlessness. I put myself in Nhi's shoes and realized we are each others mirrors. (Karen Tribble).

Another student in her late fifties interviewed a Jewish woman from South America.

I rediscovered, through Vera's eyes and expressions, my own fortuitous re-entry into the academic world. Vera's account of the impact of U.S. culture on her life served to crystallize what I, myself, had discovered about this country; that the country could be discovered only through a subjective prism within myself and my subconscious world. In terms of my ESL teaching, the cultural thread permeating this study has given me, too, new insights. Women are women everywhere, men are men and children's lives are universal and belong to tomorrow. I am grateful to Vera for my new self-awareness which reached a higher level than before the ethnography (Hannah Schild).

Ethnographers also learn about their usual communication style by comparing it with their interview style, e.g., "Do I usually take the time to know someone else? Am I fragmented or superficial in my discussion with people? Are the discussions public or private? Am I a talker or a good listener or both? Students in the TESOL program mentioned above made these comments about conducting an ethnographic interview:

Throughout, the tenor of our conversation fluctuated between public/factual and private/personal opinions. The conversation started in a nonreciprocal manner (e.g., my short direct questions, his lengthy answers), and ended in a forum of equal participation, in which the conversation "zig zagged" (Robert Dill).

When Gramp responded with animation (and at length) I pursued the topic. I felt a little ashamed of myself for not delving into his feelings about much of anything—ever before. Subsequently, I probed a bit into his feelings about the recent move. His shyness because of his hearing problem and aching knees made me realize that I need to *listen* to him more and not tell him, "You *have* to get out and make friends." I sensed that I must have greater empathy and try to understand his trepidation in his current situation rather than feeling annoyed when he fails to "push" himself. The talk was an eye opener for me (Terry O'Meara).

A friend had pointed out that, because of the personal strife I had experienced in the past year or two, I had become rather self-involved and was a much better talker than a listener. I hoped that the experience of *really* listening to someone would help. . . . What has made the biggest impression on me as I have done this ethnography is how right my friend is. Listening is a wonderful gift, one that should not be denied to others, especially a friend, if you really want to understand that person and be a friend, as well as have one (Kathleen Kwiatkowski).

The examples speak for themselves.

The effects of being a "participant"

In positively relating to members of another culture, awareness of the differences or even of one's own ethnocentrism may not be enough to overcome the differences, as we will see in the next chapter. While such awareness may provide an important step in the process, it is the ethnographer's role as *participant* that adds a critical component to overcoming the barriers, just as it is the informant's participation that influences his/her own rapport with the ethnographer. Mutual participation of both the observer and the observed distinguishes ethnography from other methods. As stressed in Chapter 5, only two-way treatments can remedy crosscultural misunderstandings. Ultimately, cultural barriers are not found in the target culture nor one's own. Rather they are a function of the distance between the two. To the extent that ethnographers get inside the picture, participate, integrate, and interpret the new cultural experiences, the barriers between themselves and the other culture will be decreased.

Conclusion

In conclusion, doing ethnography constitutes a valuable tool for facilitating positive impressions and interactions between people of different cultures. It provides a method of obtaining information about different cultures, from the cultural actor's point of view, and a method of evaluating whether crosscultural goals are reflected in classroom practices. Such evaluation may then diagnose specific areas in need of educational treatment if the goals are to be fulfilled. Of equal importance, doing ethnography provides a process for facilitating interaction and promoting friendships between people of different cultures. Therefore, students and teachers of other languages and cultures would benefit by doing ethnography as part of their studies and training.

Chapter 7

How can we modify negative perceptions of other people?
A social learning theory approach

As we saw in Chapter 5, once negative impressions are formed, they are difficult to change. To reiterate, the best solution is to build positive impressions from the beginning. However, the latter is not always possible. This chapter now focuses on how we can modify negative perceptions once they are formed.

The practices of language educators and crosscultural trainers tend to reflect the idea that prediction or anticipation of what is to come can help cushion culture shock, even if what is to come is perceived as negative differences. For example, Seelye (1978) in *Teaching Culture* asserts that crosscultural understanding will take place as students learn *what* to expect in certain circumstances and *why* it is reasonable from the target society's point of view. Hence, even seemingly negative behaviours, such as eating snakes, being continually touched, or not keeping a promise should be better tolerated.

This chapter presents a different perspective. This chapter suggests that predictability of a target cultural event, based on knowledge alone, may actually increase negative perceptions unless the learner has mastered the skills to cope with the event. Psychological research suggests that predictability of an event perceived as negative may cause greater anxiety than no predictability at all. That is, awareness that a bad thing is going to happen may cause greater anxiety than no prior knowledge, if the perceiver has not learned to cope with or control the event. Without the learner's confidence that "I can cope with it," the learner may put up greater defences and fight the event or avoid it altogether. Both are results of feeling inadequate to deal with the known, predicted differences.

Overcoming something negative or feared about another person or cultural event is, in a sense, like getting over a phobia. It involves behavior modification. Social learning theory offers approaches to coping with events perceived as negative which may be useful to second language and crosscultural educators.[1]

Predictability: culture shock or culture cushion?

The psychological literature regarding the effects of predictability on anxiety is somewhat conflicting. Initial studies seemed to show that being able to predict that a bad thing is going to happen is better than no predictability at all (Zimbardo and Ruch, 1977; Seligman, 1968; Badia, Culbertson and Harch, 1973). These studies explain that predictability reduces uncertainty, thereby reducing anxiety. However, these studies have often confounded general predictability with the issue of *when*.

That is, the experimental subjects have been able to predict *when* the bad thing was going to happen, as opposed to only *if* it was going to happen at all. For example, in one study two groups of rats were shocked daily at random intervals, during a period of 45 days. However, one group always heard a buzzer before they were shocked, so they knew when the bad event was coming. Both groups could predict they were going to be shocked, so neither group represented a no predictability group. The only difference is that the second group could also predict when they were safe; they were less anxious during the periods between buzzers (Seligman, 1968),

In another study, male college volunteer subjects were shocked approximately every 45 seconds. In a second part of the study, the shock remained as often and as intense, but the rest period was preceded by a signal indicating that relief was on the way. According to the researchers, "the subjects' blood pressure dropped markedly as soon as the signal appeared" (Hokanson, DeGood, Forrest and Brittain, 1971). While this study is cited as evidence for the benefits of predictability over no predictability, again the study lacked a no-predictability group. Both groups predicted that the bad event—a shock—was going to happen. The signal predicted the positive event, namely, cessation of shock.

Other studies confuse predictability with control. For example, two groups of rats were again shocked daily. However, the second group had a bar in their cage to stop the shock. For the second group, after a buzzer sounded, the rats had a few seconds in which to push the bar to prevent the shock from occurring. Not surprisingly, once the second group learned to push the bar, they had much less anxiety than the other group because they could control it. They could also predict periods of safety. As in the other studies, this study lacked a no predictability group.

There is little empirical evidence to conclude that general predictability of negatively-perceived events will make these preferred over unpredictable ones.

Learned helplessness: predictability with no control

Recent research which has carefully separated predictability from control suggests that general predictability of a negative event may itself increase stress and anxiety (Miller and Grant, 1978).

One study about predictability and human stress identified two types of people: those who want information about negative events to come, and those who do not. Subjects were able to choose between tuning into a signal which predicted a negative event or listening to music. The negative event occurred regardless of the subjects' choice; they were not able to control it. Results indicated that the people who wanted the negative information were more stressed than those who listened to the music (Miller, 1978b).

Knowing a bad thing is to come and not knowing what to do about it may be akin to "learned helplessness," a term coined by the psychologist, Seligman, 1968. Consider the following example of an American man in Guatemala:

You see all these people? They're all my wife's relatives. And every damn one of them has kissed me tonight. If another Guatemalan man hugs and kisses me, I'll punch him right in the face (Seelye, 1978).

Seelye cites this story as an example of "cultural fatigue." In the above example, the American's hostility derived from his actual experience with the event he perceived as negative and his awareness or prediction that it would recur. With each recurrence the American may have learned helplessness.

Helplessness is defined in terms of the uncontrolability of probable events. A study involving learned helplessness in dogs illustrates the debilitating effect of no control situations on future learning. One group of dogs were put into harnesses, then shocked without any control or time signal. Later these dogs were put into a compartment and trained to jump a barrier to avoid shock, but two-thirds of them could not learn to jump the barrier. Another group of dogs, who had not been previously shocked, quickly learned to jump the barrier (Seligman, 1975).

Another study replicated this helplessness experiment with college students. In the first part of the study, two groups of students were exposed to loud noise. For one group, the noise was inescapable. The second group had an escape condition in which they were able to control the noise. In the second part of the study, the same two groups plus another group (who had not been exposed to noise at all) were put into the following experiment:

The three groups were then taken to a finger shuttle box in which a loud noise occurred when a finger was placed on one side of the box, but ceased when the finger was moved to the other side. It was found that both the escape and no-noise group subjects learned to turn the noise off by moving their hands to the other side of the shuttlebox, while the subjects who had experienced the inescapable condition did not escape the noise, but remained passive (Hiroto, 1974).

Learned helplessness may lead to a generalized belief of "can't do," which in turn affects subsequent efforts: "the motivation to respond is sapped, the ability to perceive success is undermined, and emotionality is heightened" (Seligman, 1975).

Foreign-language students, Peace Corps volunteers, and language minorities in bilingual classrooms may experience a sense of learned helplessness in target cultural situations, real or simulated.

In a study of foreign-language students, American college students attending a six-week French summer school were examined for their feelings of anomie and authoritarianism at the start and end of the course. Elementary language level and advanced language level groups were included. The students, who had promised to speak only French, reverted to English towards the end. Anomie also *increased* for both groups at the program's end. The researchers suggest that increases in anomie reflected increases in social dissatisfaction (Lambert and Tucker, 1972).

Many Peace Corps volunteers have enthusiastically gone into the field, only to leave frustrated and anxious. The following is an account of such volunteers in the Philippines.

The volunteers often expressed extreme frustration and sometimes hostility because it became obvious to them that the tasks which they came to accomplish so earnestly did not matter to the Filipinos (Fuchs, 1967).

Language minority students in bilingual classrooms may also experience a sense of helplessness with increased awareness of target cultural values which appear inaccessible to them. Several studies have suggested that under-achievement, poor reading, and negative attitudes to schooling are related to minority children's perceived blocked access to the rewards which accompany achievement (King, 1974, McDermott, 1974, Rosenfeld, 1971). McDermott's study of Black children who "learned not to read" in Chapter 4 is an example of how perceived blocked access and lack of internal control may cause rejection of the value itself.

In all of the above examples, hostility, frustration and anomie may be due to the absence (real or believed) of ability to control/cope with the situation and a resulting sense of helplessness.

Need for control or coping strategies

As we have seen, uncontrolability of an event, actual or believed, causes anxiety. The reverse also appears to be true: one's actual ability to control or cope with an event as well as the potential control or belief of "can do" alone will decrease stress. The following case of a hypochondriac who is afraid he is going to die of a heart attack illustrates this point. The man's heart is in good shape, but his constant anxiety is bad for his circulatory system.

He is momentarily concerned and stops to think about his heart. After introspecting deeply for a moment, he detects what he thinks might be a slight irregularity in heartbeat. . . . After he consults a psychiatrist, a tranquilizer is prescribed. He is told that the medicine is a very powerful drug and will stop his anxiety even at the height of an attack. He carries the drug in his chest pocket wherever he goes; no anxiety attack reappears. He has never taken the drug (Seligman, 1975).

In the above example, the hypochondriac believes that he has potential control over his anxiety. Another study on the relationship between urban stress and controlability showed similar effects:

It was demonstrated that subjects' belief that they could turn off an uncontrolably loud noise resulted in better performance on proofreading and problem-solving tasks than that of helpless subjects. Performance was also better when subjects believed that a person who could turn off the noise was accessible—*even though the noise was not turned off* (Glass and Singer, 1972).

Social learning theory explains that people's judgment about their potential ability to cope with a negative situation actually effects efforts to cope and subsequent actual success or failure. Within the context of crosscultural encounters, people's beliefs that they can cope with target cultural events will affect their subsequent efforts and actual ability to cope. In this regard, volunteers in Peace Corps training programs who judged that they would be able to cope in the field actually stayed longer than those who judged that they would not be able to cope.

Types of coping strategies

If a situation is perceived as threatening, there are three possible strategies for coping:

(1) *fight*—taking direct action against the situation;
(2) *flight*—escaping the situation;
(3) *benign reappraisal*—reinterpreting the situation as less threatening (Zimbardo and Ruch, 1977).

The first two strategies are accompanied by negative emotion. Only the third actually reduces the negative emotion.

In most psychological studies of control, as those cited in the previous section, control usually means flight: some form of instrumental control device like a button by which animals escape shock or people escape noise (or at least think they can). In the case of crosscultural encounters, people do not have instrumental control devices to terminate negative situations, although they may use other forms of flight: Peace Corps volunteers may leave the country of fieldwork; students of a foreign language avoid contact with native speakers of the language or refuse to speak the language. In the reduction of culture shock, we are more concerned with coping as benign reappraisal—a strategy by which we learn to cope with rather than escape from the cultural event.

Internal versus external control

When people believe that the origin of control is within themselves, they are less anxious than when control is mediated externally. For example, people who have a button to stop a shock can endure the shock longer than people who know they can call for help to someone else who has the controlling button. In the former case, less anxiety may occur because of the belief that relief is stable. This idea may be applied to anxiety related to potentially negative cultural behaviors, e.g., being spoken to in a louder voice or in closer proximity than accustomed. People who believe they have no control of the effects may interpret the situation as, "They're encroaching on my space." They believe they have no mechanism for relief and may experience acute hostility. People who do believe they have control and attribute the effects of events to themselves may say, "My standard is inapplicable here." These people, who believe that relief is within themselves, may experience benign reappraisal, assessing the situation as less threatening.

The critical question for crosscultural educators becomes, "How does one learn to reinterpret a situation as less threatening?" Social learning psychologists suggest that coping with a negative event involves active mastery. Mastery acts like a vaccine against learned helplessness.

Learning to cope through mastery: a social learning theory approach

In learning to cope, the first question which emerges is: What are we coping with? Is the concern of crosscultural educators to help students change attitudes or change behaviors? Social learning theory suggests that behavioral change leads to atttitude change. "One cannot treat abstractions. It is thoughts, affective expressions, and actions which are modified" (Bandura, 1978).

In the context of bilingual, foreign language and crosscultural training programs, there are frequent reactions against specification of behavioral objectives. Opponents criticize that in these contexts behavioral objectives are often too narrowly defined, and refer to learning about discrete customs or habits within the target culture. While such criticisms may be valid, behavioral objectives need not be so narrowly defined. In social learning terms, behavioral objectives refer to a broader context. They refer to recognizable expressions which include physiological responses, evaluative reactions and judgments. For example, an American student of Japanese may experience a negative behavioral reaction to a breakfast of raw egg and seaweed. A negative physiological urge may be accompanied by an evaluative "ugh," (whether verbalized or not). A British student of Italian may respond similarly to a conversation with a native speaker which is louder, spatially closer, and more personal than what s/he is accustomed to. The behavioral reaction of the American in Guatemala cited earlier included a desire to physically punch the next greeter, a negative emotion and a probable negative judgment about his wife's relatives!

Social learning theory offers an approach to modifying such negative behavioral reactions which begins with indirect experience via a model, i.e., observational learning, and then proceeds to direct learner experience through guided participation.

"Modeling" in social learning terms does *not* mean mere presentation of the behavior followed by learner imitation. Successful modeling which leads to skill mastery involves six critical conditions:

(1) a psychological match between the learner, the model and the modeled event,
(2) learners' perception that the model is similar to themselves,
(3) experience with a variety of models, multiple observations and trials with the threatening situation,
(4) learner observation of positive consequences related to the potentially negative situation,
(5) repeated exposure to tasks which are graduated over time, and last long enough to overcome initial anxiety,
(6) learner self-efficacy judgments, i.e., that s/he "can do .. can cope" with the event.

Each of these conditions will be further elaborated below.

Psychological matching

People must be able to understand modeled opinions and behaviors if they are to be influenced by them. Psychological matching means that the modeled event matches the learner in terms of skills complexity, function of the behavior, and value perceived by the observer. This idea is akin to the discussion in Chapter 3 which focused on learning as a process of building bridges from the known to the unknown and stressed the importance of using culturally and personally familiar events as the point of departure.

Let us pretend that our learners are afraid to enter a culture where everyone is a gymnast of Olympic standards, and they will be expected to participate in a group run of 5 miles each morning, at 8 minutes a mile. The learners' present physical skill level does not exceed $\frac{1}{2}$ mile in 10 minutes. Learner observation of the 5-mile run, at 8 minutes a mile, will not match their present skill complexity, and will do little to stimulate mastery, since it is not perceived as within their grasp. Observations of models who run $\frac{1}{2}$ mile in 10 minutes, gradually increasing their speed and length, will be more effective. In this regard, second language educators may begin to question the idea that beginning with a normal flow of speech is the most effective point of departure to accustom a beginning student's ear to the sounds of the new language.

Learners will also pay more attention to the modeled behavior if the task matches their interests or needs; that is, if they perceive the task as personally relevant or if they expect to perform a similar task. For example, in developing empathy towards members of a particular sect, it is pointless to model a snake-handling ceremony just because it is culturally authentic, if it is unlikely the learners will be confronted with that situation. Before deciding which target cultural events to deal with, crosscultural educators may want to consider which target cultural situations are relevant to their students and which are presented for the sake of knowledge alone, at the risk of underscoring differences.

On the other hand, if, say, it is likely that the sect's handling of snakes may contribute to negative perceptions of sect members and inhibit positive interaction, then the event is better dealt with (even though learners may never have to directly handle snakes). In order to provide a psychological match with the function of the event, modeling of handling other, more known animals, such as dogs or cats, would be a more effective point of departure. In other words, replication of target cultural events *per se* may be less effective than initial presentation of modified behaviors which provide greater matches with learners. While some aspects of the modeled behaviour will necessarily be new, they must also match some existing skills, functions, and values within the learner.

Similarity of the model

Models whom learners perceive as similar to themselves provide greater psychological matches and therefore influence learning more than those who are perceived as dissimilar.

Ordinarily, people favor reference models similar to their own ability over highly divergent ones whose behavior they can match only through great effort (Bandura, 1978).

This idea reinforces the last discussion in Chapter 5 regarding perceived similarity and affiliation.

Model similarity also refers to the idea of "similarly threatened." If we see models as in the same boat, we are more likely to learn from them. Kazdin (1974) found that observations of fearful, similar models gradually overcoming their fears helps subjects reduce fears and exhibit coping behaviour more than watching models with no fear behave in a threatened situation. This idea of model similarity has serious, if not startling implications for cultural modeling in classes aimed at reducing negative responses to a particular cultural group. This would suggest that models perceived as more similar to learners might be more effective *in initial stages of learning* than models chosen solely on the basis of cultural authenticity, language proficiency and expertise. Non-members of the target culture who can appropriately and sympathetically model the given behavior may be equally or more beneficial to fulfill the conditions of psychological match and similarity at the beginning stages of adaptation.

Variety of models and observation trials

A variety of models and observation trials offers more opportunities for potential matches with learners. Through the process of modeling, observers select various aspects of different models and synthesize them. Modeling in the context of social learning theory is not mere imitation, but rather a process of innovative psychological matching. Crosscultural educators may introduce students to a variety of models through films, visitors, team teaching, peer teaching, and teaching by students who have successfully completed the course or are in the next level.

A variety of models is also motivating to learners, who may reason, "If a variety of people like me can do that, why can't I?".

Observation of positive consequences

Modeling of an event which learners fear is more likely to have a positive effect if the learner observes consequences which are positive. By seeing models performing feared activities without any harmful effects, the learner's defensive behavior is weakened and fear is reduced. Positive feedback and praise are also important factors.

People will adopt high performance standards that reduce self-gratification, they will select nonpreferred foods, they will divulge personal problems, and they will pursue formerly resisted courses of action more readily if they see models praised for exhibiting such conduct than if models receive no recognition for their action (Bandura, 1977, p. 119).

The above example seems particularly applicable to crosscultural encounters in which students may be confronted with things they potentially resist.

Repeated exposure to graduated tasks

We have all heard the truism, "Things take time." Chapter 4 suggested that cultural behaviors are acquired through repeated exposure. Similarly, social learning theory stresses that behavioral change also takes time, with gradual approaches to the new goal, in steps. For a man who has a fear of height, the worst approach is to immediately send him to the top of the tallest tower. Throwing a person who cannot swim into a swimming pool, if not causing drowning, will likely cause a lifelong fear of the water. The old adage, "sink or swim" is psychologically devastating. If "necessity is the mother of invention," in certain circumstances it is also the mother of subsequent negative reactions and defensive behavior.

Social learning theory suggests that even the model should not immediately perform the feared behavior, but should approach it in stages. First learners observe, then they jointly participate with the model, and eventually they perform the task on their own.

The timing of tasks should also be graduated. It is easier to begin enduring a feared event for brief periods of time. Gradually, the time should be increased. However, it is important that even initial periods are long enough to work through stress, which increases initially. Short sessions produce more distress.

These principles may apply to any cultural behavior perceived as negative, e.g., someone perceived as shouting, someone perceived as overpersonal, someone perceived as cold, or eating disliked foods. They may even apply to speaking the language itself, if the learner perceives the situation as embarrassing and difficult. Through observation of the model, gradually approaching the feared behaviour, to actual joint performance of the feared behavior, over increasingly longer periods of time, people learn to cope with events they initially feared or perceived as negative.

Learners "can do" judgments

Positive judgments about one's own ability actually cause increased efforts in future situations, which influences actual subsequent success. People learn to believe in themselves by mastery, by feedback, and by setting up internal standards and rewards.

To coin yet another saying, "Nothing succeeds like success!" When people master the skills necessary to cope and actually experience success, their positive judgment about their ability to cope in future situations increases. Mastery is accomplished through the conditions discussed in the foregoing sections. Learners judge their own degree of mastery by various criteria:

(1) *difficulty of the task*: Learners have greater feelings of success by accomplishing tasks they perceive as difficult than those they perceive as easy.

(2) *amount of effort and time expended*: The less effort it takes for learners to accomplish the task, the greater their feelings of success.

(3) *amount of external aid received*: The less aid received, the greater are learner feelings of mastery.

(4) *situational circumstances*: The more difficult the situation, the greater learner belief in their ability.

(5) *emotional arousal*: The less anxiety learners feel while accomplishing the task, the better they feel about their ability (Bandura, 1978).

In other words, a football player who makes a touchdown at the beginning of a game, against a tough team, in a field muddy from the rain, will feel more capable than one who plays in optimal conditions against an easy team.

People also learn about their success through feedback from others, Like any problem solving activity, learning to cope through taking on new behaviors requires verification of accuracy: "Is my behavior accurate? Are my standards appropriate?" The new behavior may be verified directly or indirectly. Direct feedback from teachers influences feelings of success or lack of it. Indirectly, learners may observe the consequences of someone else's actions, e.g., the model's. Students of another culture may deduce their accuracy from the reaction of other people met in crosscultural encounters. Students' subsequent efforts to speak or tolerate a cultural behavior perceived as threatening will be influenced by the reaction. A compliment about a student's conversation ability or other positive reaction from a native speaker goes a long way toward making a student feel successful and stimulating continued efforts which lead to actual mastery. It is for this reason that I teach my students to be "language bluffs" immediately: they learn to say a few things fluently with appropriate nonverbal behaviors from the first day and try them out on the first native speaker they encounter. They are generally rewarded by the native speaker and motivated to continue. Until greater mastery is achieved, the catch is they must make a quick exit from the encounter after the short, albeit superficial exchange is completed to avoid bewilderment and embarrassment by a subsequent onslaught of incomprehensible speech!

Learners also verify their behavior by comparing it with the judgment of others. One's peer group plays a particularly important role in this comparison through social cueing. In the study of student impressions of foreign people mentioned in Chapter 5, one frequent criticism was that Italians were "abrupt" (Robinson, 1981). In a later training session, students were asked how they judged "abruptness." The manner in which students began responding was particularly interesting. First, one hand was raised. Then two. Within minutes, a chain reaction was occurring and hands were waving across the room, as in the manner of applauding after a second curtain call at the theatre. This manner of responding alone is an example of social cueing. More importantly, in a similar chain reaction fashion, negative judgments about foreign people changed to neutral judgments. An interesting finding occurred involving the few students who responded to an open-ended questionnaire *after* this training session (rather than before, as with the other students). When asked to describe their impressions of people from foreign countries, they were the only seventh grade students in the school to respond neutrally, with the comment, "Can't judge."

A social learning interpretation of the findings suggests that investigator modeling, guided participation and subsequent peer cueing influenced actual behavior and feedback as to appropriate behaviors. Through guided participation, students discovered their own linguistic behaviors and their own system of evaluating abruptness. Defensive reactions to not understanding other people's communicative standards were inhibited as students learned where the misunderstandings occurred. Through social cueing the norm among the peer group no longer supported a negative judgment of people with different linguistic standards in general, nor in reference to the Italians in particular.

In the above study it is likely that student defensiveness and belief in their inability to effectively communicate influenced how they behaved toward the Italians, and how the Italians behaved toward them. Conversely, positive judgments about other people influence our positive beliefs about coping with them, our positive behavior toward them, and their behavior toward us.

Lastly, learners' "can do" judgments are influenced by their own internal standards of success and system of rewards. As we saw earlier, perceived control within the individual is the most effective cushion against anxiety. Through a social learning theory approach to mastery, learners go through a process of self-correction and learn to regulate their own behavior through an internal system of rewards. Learners gradually correct and modify their own behavior until it matches the modeled behavior. They set up an internal standard for what accurate match means.

When learners are themselves able to set up goals or standards to attain, correct their own behavior until they reach it, and reward themselves, the chances for continued success or maintenance of the behavior are greater. Therefore, it is important that bilingual, second language and crosscultural educators organize instruction in such a way that students set up attainment goals, engage in self-correction and self-rewards.

Contrasts with other crosscultural sensitization approaches

As we have seen, social learning theory suggests that modifying negative perceptions about people from other cultures involves modifying one's own behavior. Through various conditions and stages of modeling, learners observe, participate, and eventually master the threatened behavior, giving them internal control over reactions toward it. Learners have multiple chances to gradually approach the threatening situation, with the help of a model who is similar to themselves, in a situation which has positive consequences, resulting in a "can do" opinion about themselves *vis-à-vis* the once threatening situation. In contrast, many approaches to lessening culture shock are marked by awareness alone, or one-time, short exercises in which students experience hostility and embarrassment in the name of cultural sensitization.

Awareness through lecturing and reading

One common approach to preparing students for culture shock situations is simply to tell students about the things which may cause the greatest problems, i.e., the differences, and provide readings on the subject. This creates a general predictability of the negative event which, as we have seen, may cause anxiety, fight or flight.

Self-confrontation: mini-dramas

Another approach is the mini-drama as suggested by Gorden, 1970. The mini-drama consists of from three to five brief episodes, each of which contains one or more examples of miscommunication. A discussion led by the teacher follows each episode. The purpose of the mini-drama is to provide cultural information and to evoke an emotional response which results in self-confrontation (Seelye, 1978, pp. 91–92). A discussion follows each episode. After the initial episode, guilt is usually attributed to the foreigner. After several episodes later, participants change their opinion and attribute guilt to the American. Seelye explains his use of this technique in the crosscultural training of foreign language teachers:

By identifying with the Americans of the drama and by misinterpreting the same cultural cues, the teachers had almost experienced the embarrassment of a cultural *faux pas*. The emotional sensitivity came from knowing that they were all vulnerable to lack of empathy (Seelye, 1978).

The above approach is quite different from a social learning approach, which ensures success each step of the way. In the mini-drama, participants experience failure and embarrassment rather than a successful coping attempt. While learners' sensitivity may well be increased, it is questionable that feelings of "can do" will be enhanced. The mini-drama is also different from the social learning approach in that each mini-drama is a short presentation, which is presented only once and which does not directly end in positive consequences.

Role play and cultural simulations

Role play exercises and cultural simulations are contrasted with social learning theory in many of the same respects. Role play exercises are like the example of immediately sending the man afraid of height to the top of the tower. There is rarely a similar model, no gradual approach to the goal, and no multiple trials for psychological matching to occur.

BAFA BAFA is a cultural simulation in which students are divided into two fictitious groups: the alphas and the betas. Each group is given a set of tasks to perform and rules for social interaction. However, these rules are unknown to the other group. Then the groups attempt to interact. The betas are only interested in exchanging cards in order to obtain a full set. The alphas know nothing of this goal; instead, their goal is to make friends.

A debriefing of 15 to 50 minutes generally follows the game, which is played once and lasts about an hour. During a debriefing session of university students who played BAFA BAFA at the University of California, Berkeley, and the University of Santa Clara, participants were asked to describe their opinions about the other cultural group. Negative adjectives such as "aggressive, hostile," were used by the alphas to describe the betas. "Lazy, uncooperative" were adjectives used by the betas to describe the alphas. Students described their own reactions as "frustrated, anxious, hostile."

The simulation developers state that the purpose of the game is to simulate culture shock, a goal which is generally fulfilled! They maintain that experiencing culture shock prior to field experience will cushion actual shock by increasing awareness of crosscultural problems. Social learning theorists might even question these cognitive gains owing to the lack of specific, real behaviors which are dealt with in the model of fictitious cultures. Notwithstanding the latter, the assumption here again is that predictability of a negative event will lessen anxiety.

No research has evaluated the relationship among such cultural shock simulations, learner "can do" judgements about coping in the target culture, and actual ability to cope in crosscultural encounters. According to social learning theory, such simulations may contribute to learned helplessness: shocking without mastering how to cope. The experience is similar to subjects in helplessness experiments who could not escape the noise. Participants are thrown into an anxious shock situation. They are given no cues as to how to handle interaction. They have no means of controlling either the negative situation or their negative reactions to it.

While such approaches may be less beneficial than is assumed for helping students to successfully cope when they are the newcomer in a foreign situation, they may serve other valuable functions in crosscultural training. By experiencing such helplessness, participants, such as bilingual and ESL teachers may become sensitized to the helplessness of people from different linguistic and ethnic backgrounds when confronted with a totally new and foreign situation.

Other approaches to crosscultural sensitization are abundant, particularly in the literature on intercultural communication. The examples above serve only to provide marked contrasts with social learning theory so the latter may be more fully understood.

Conclusion

Many approaches to modifying negative perceptions of people from other cultures stress awareness and/or immediate experiences of the threatening situation, via mini-dramas, role play or simulations. The assumption is that as learners become aware of what to expect in crosscultural encounters, they should be able to respond more positively. This chapter has suggested that prediction or anticipation of a negative event may decrease one's actual ability to cope with the situation. Modifying negative perceptions of other people involves modifying one's own behavior. Change the behavior and the attitude will follow. Second language, foreign language, bilingual and crosscultural educators may gain valuable insights by applying the principles of social learning theory to crosscultural adaptation strategies. Learners' positive beliefs in their own ability to cope with the new situation result from mastery. Mastery can be achieved through successful modeling which proceeds from indirect to direct experience according to several critical conditions: the behaviors modeled should not overtax the learner in skill complexity; the behaviors should have observable positive consequences; there should be multiple observational trials and models; the tasks should be repeated and graduated over time; the model should be similar to the learner in some way and similarly threatened as a point of departure. Each of these conditions provides psychological matches between the learner, the modeled event and the model.

While the foregoing discussion is theoretically based, future research is needed to evaluate social learning approaches to crosscultural understanding, after programs which incorporate such approaches have been developed and taught.

Note

1 The area of "values clarification theory" is also pertinent to the discussion in this chapter. Educators have suggested that awareness and clarification of one's own values and the values of others promotes positive interaction. The discussion of values clarification theory will be left to specialists in that area (e.g., Coombs, 1971; Meux, 1971); however, the discussion in this chapter should suggest new questions for values education, such as, "To what extent does clarifying one's own values and the values of people from different cultures influence interaction with people whose cultural values are perceived as different?"

Chapter 8

Becoming multicultural

Multicultural man: myth or reality?

Cultural pluralism is a reality of the twentieth century. Some say that multicultural man is equally a reality. The latter is debatable.

The conditions of contemporary history are such that we may now be on the threshold of a new kind of person, a person who is socially and psychologically a product of the interweaving of cultures in the twentieth century (Adler, 1976, p. 362).

While the conditions of history point to the potential and need for multicultural man, dominant modes of interaction still reflect monoculturalism. In Sydney, London, Tokyo, Memphis, and San Francisco, people tend to live in geographic clusters, among their own; children play on playgrounds in culturally mixed schools, among their own, e.g., Anglo Australians separated from Greeks, Japanese separated from Koreans, British from Indians, American Blacks from Whites and Anglos from Chicanos. On university campuses in the United States, student activities and interactions often center around fraternities, sororities and ethnic houses dominated by monocultural interests. University courses designed to teach about cultural diversity often function monoculturally in terms of classroom interaction patterns, criteria for acceptable student responses and indicators of success. At the culturally and racially pluralistic apartment complex where I live in California, people talk, swim and play tennis primarily with people like themselves.

Living, playing and interacting among one's own are not inherently bad habits; indeed, they may be inherently natural. The study of anthropology gives credence to the saying, "birds of a feather flock together." There is a tendency toward group maintenance, not only for human groups but for groups of animals in the wild. Primates interact not only in species groups, but by subclass. Spider monkeys and gibbons live in separate herds; they develop hierarchies and social divisions among themselves.

Even if one accepts the idea that ethnocentrism is a natural tendency, we intervene in natural tendencies to make life better all the time. We irrigate land where there is no natural rainfall. We cure some natural diseases with medicine. From this perspective we could probably also overcome ethnocentrism if we think the benefits are worth it.

There are features of the twentieth century which require intercultural contact.

Communication and cultural exchange are the pre-eminent conditions of the twentieth century. For the first time in the history of the world, a patchwork of technology and organization has made possible simultaneous interpersonal and intercultural communication (Ibid., p. 363).

Not only is culture contact a reality brought about through modernization, communications and urbanization, but also a reality of local, national and planetary functioning. No other period in history has been so marked by the need to foster interdependence and positive interactions among people of diverse ethnic and linguistic groups. Rivers has poignantly noted the trends that are developing.

Two divergent trends are becoming very evident on the national and international scene: interdependence and assertion of identity. Both are potential sources of tension and conflict.... In our educational institutions, we must prepare students for concord and productive living in a world where these two forces are determining the social and political environment in which they live and work.... Essential to harmonious living in such a world will be the ability to comprehend others.... Our citizens must learn to live with such diversity (Rivers, 1981).

Developing cultural versatility

This book has explored the dilemma of reducing such conflict and living with diversity from an individual perspective. It has posed the questions, "How can a person from one culture understand someone from another? What approaches may help a person feel comfortable with and interact positively with someone who appears culturally different?" In exploring the processes and approaches from psychological and anthropological perspectives, it has become evident that crosscultural understanding involves more than knowledge of how and why other people think and behave as they do. To reiterate the beginning quote of this book:

It's nonsense to think that learning about cultural diversity will bring about acceptance of it—the effect can be to increase bias. It's nonsense to think that understanding and acceptance is essentially a cognitive process (Coladarci, 1976).

Understanding someone from another culture involves modifying one's own cultural repertoire; i.e., developing cultural versatility. Throughout the book this idea has emerged through a variety of processes.

Summary of processes

Cognitive psychology taught us that we can only see someone else's point of view from our own vantage point. Our own past experience, both individual and cultural, influences how what we perceive and how we think about things. The study of culture itself disclosed that it involves internal processes of organizing the world and dynamic processes of creating meaning, as well as ways of behaving and rules for behaving. Analyses of cultural acquisition showed that culture is acquired, not only through the process of reason, but through all the senses, even though cultures influence which senses may be more dominant. Equally important, culture is acquired within an integrated context; i.e., when an integrated set of signals conveys the same message.

Studies of person perception disclosed that positive interaction takes place when perceptions match, through every perceptual mode. Psychological matching implies similarity. People perceive different people more similarly when they focus on similarities, find similarities beneath the differences, and become more like the other people, and vice versa.

Analyses of ethnography indicated that the process of doing ethnography can help promote positive perceptions by being with another person over time, listening and developing self-awareness. As participants, observers and interpreters, ethnographers negotiate between the target culture and their own, thereby gaining a more authentic vantage point on the culture studied.

Person perception studies also taught us that perceiving others positively is a difficult task because people are not always rational in processing information. Differences stand out more perceptually, and once we have a particular frame of reference, it is difficult to change. According to social learning theory, changing cultural attitudes means changing cultural behaviors; i.e., behavioral modification. Modifying behavior takes place gradually, over time.

Each process above underscored the idea that learning begins at home; i.e., cultural learning proceeds from the known to the unknown. Since no one can be a cultural or perceptual *tabula rasa*, any authentic product of cultural learning will be a synthesis. Synthesis indicates change; in this case, cultural change, cultural versatility.

Contrast with approaches in foreign language, second language and bilingual programs

In contrast with the above processes and their implied approaches, cultural instruction does not usually build bridges between the home and target culture. Typically, cultural instruction begins with that which is unique or different about the culture of study. Material is usually presented verbally and visually without the stimulation of emotion or other senses. Instruction is aimed at knowledge and awareness of how and why other people act the way they do, even though this information may increase bias. Foreign and second language texts are filled with discrete exercises. Students are asked to role play and imitate the target behavior rather than synthesize it with their own experience. Foreign language programs often approach the target culture from perspectives independent of those of the learners. Conversely, bilingual education may teach language minorities about their own culture, independent of the mainstream. Rarely do mainstream and minorities learn about each other and learn to feel comfortable with each other's language and cultural behavior.

These approaches differ markedly from those that may lead to changing the way a learner perceives, feels and behaves toward someone from another culture.

Becoming multicultural: subtractive biculturalism, marginality or versatility?

When we modify our ways of perceiving to include a variety of perspectives, we are in a sense, becoming multicultural. As such, the distance between them and us decreases.

Some people view becoming multicultural as a threat to individual identity. One argument is akin to that of subtractive bilingualism. It tends to be based on observations of people who have had to modify their cultural identity to survive; e.g., immigrants in a new country, cultural minorities, and citizens whose country has come under outside domination. In many cases, these people have had to give up or subordinate their own cultural identity in order to succeed within the dominant or dominating culture.

Another argument points to the marginality of people who have successfully expanded their repertoires by living abroad and subsequently find themselves living on the boundaries, like a man without a country. They have no in-group with whom to identify.

Cultural change from the perspective of the society or the individual need not be threatening. Individual biculturalism or multiculturalism could be expansive rather than subtractive. Cultural versatility implies expanding one's repertoire of experiences and behaviors, not subtracting anything. Marginality could be replaced by a more diverse in-group. If the principles explored in this book were taken to their logical conclusion, people from one culture would become a little bit of "other", and would have a degree of psychological match with more people. However, an individual or group's dominant cultural identity would not be threatened. Different cultural groups would only have more shared experiences; i.e., a larger degree of overlap, as pictured below.

Unlike for the isolated marginal man, if everyone were on the boundary, perhaps it would not be such a lonely place to be.

Some say the threat of such multiculturalism does not lie in identity but in economy and power. Some anthropologists and educational economists argue that cultural and social class boundaries, i.e., tight in-group/out-group divisions, serve political and economic functions. They suggest that schooling itself functions to maintain culture and reproduce social class structures (Carnoy and Levin, 1976; Spindler, 1974). Schooling may also function to change culture, to diversify class structures, and lessen conflict.

People-made culture is the principal lesson of modern anthropology; people can remake it . . . (Dolgin *et al.*, 1977).

Discussion of identity, acculturalism and power is like opening up Pandora's box—a box I shall leave for others to explore. However, it is an essential area of consideration in the establishment and fulfilment of crosscultural goals. Ultimately, implementation of approaches that will lead to the breaking down of cultural barriers will hinge on such consideration and related decisions.

Conclusion

The time has come to abolish unfruitful catch phrases like, "Let's step into the shoes of the 'other' person," or "Let's see it from 'their' point of view." Such phrases lead to strategies of imitation and false hopes of total empathy or understanding. It is equally unfruitful to equate knowledge and awareness of cultural differences with human understanding. Such understanding must pervade the senses and influence behavior. Ensuring that learners' own cultural and individual experience is reflected in their multisensory responses to new cultural stimuli will certainly never lead to objectivity in viewing someone else, but it may be a critical step toward approaching "other" as part of "self." To the extent that we perceive other people as similar to ourselves, to the extent that we feel comfortable with their behaviors, and they with ours, mutually positive interactions may take place. It is in the process of developing cultural versatility, i.e., becoming a little multicultural—that the differences between people will be decreased.

Appendix: a case study of an ethnographic interview

Moon-Uncle, Moon-Uncle,
come, come, come
Here is a spinning top,
come, come, come
Here is a copper pot,
come, come, come
Here is a coconut
come, come, come
Here is a pomegranate,
come, come, come
Here is a carriage
and here is a drum,
Moon-Uncle, Moon-Uncle
come, come, come

Moon-Uncle, Moon-Uncle, why do you hide?
Why do you hide in the old neem tree?
Moon-Uncle, Moon-Uncle, come inside;
Come to my house and live with me.

Moon-Uncle, Moon-Uncle, come and eat—
roti spread with golden ghee.
A fly fell in with his dirty feet!
And a hungry moon has abandoned me.

Throughout the rhymes images of uncle appear and reappear. The uncle, especially in joint-family households, occupies a particularly powerful position, sometimes dictatorial, sometimes benevolent. It is not surprising that as important an object as the moon—and the moon seems to shine with unusual splendor in India—should be personified, much as our Mother Earth, in the form of the dominant figure in family life, "Umbili Amama" or "Chand Mama", the child calls in rhyme after rhyme: "Moon-Uncle, Moon-Uncle."

Yet for all their differences, English and Indian nursery rhymes have in common elements that seem to appeal to children the world over ... The Indian child has his moon-uncle, the Western child his man in the moon, and the only apparent difference is that the one dines on roti spread with golden ghee, the other on cold pease porridge. Long may they both dine.

(*MOON-UNCLE, MOON-UNCLE,
Rhymes from India*, translated
by Sylvia Cassedy and Parvathi
Thampi, Doubleday & Co.,
New York, 1973.)

How does it *feel* to be a student from India at Stanford?

"How does it *feel* to be a student from India at Stanford?" That's the bull's-eye question I asked another graduate student. At the most general level, the bull's-eye was chosen to provide a means of facilitating interaction and positive attitudes between students of different cultures. But why ask another student "how it feels" in order to accomplish this goal? First, the question is based on the premise that lack of interaction and negative attitudes may be related to lack of knowing, and more importantly, lack of empathizing with the other person. Lack of empathy may in turn be related to failure to recognize the commonalities. As the introductory poem conveyed, one child dines on roti spread, and the other on cold pease porridge, but when they are hungry, they both eat. However, it is the differences which are most readily perceived: we see different clothes, different body movements; we hear different accents, different linguistic codes . . . we taste foods that are "too spicy" or "too bland". Less readily perceived are the underlying commonalities, e.g. hunger, fear, love, anger, confusion. Most people experience these things, although the specific conditions which influence these states and their form of expression may differ from culture to culture. We have tended to dwell on these different conditions and the different forms of expression. But this is normal. Memory stores and retrieves information based on "distinctive" features. Differences among people are more "distinctive" than similarities, so it is not surprising that most educational programs aiming to teach about people from other cultures begin by underlining the differences. But providing information about differences without stimulating empathy may strengthen cultural barriers. Bruner and his associates (1973) came to this conclusion while working on the social studies program, *Man: a Course of Study*.

By concentrating on the information-giving aspects of films on the Eskimos, prejudice increased, but by encouraging children to try to understand the feelings, they decreased the danger of prejudice.

So my bull's-eye question was not, "what do you *think*", but "how do you *feel*" about being here. Similarly I rarely asked my informant to describe aspects of life in India. I was more interested in understanding her feelings about being here than learning about the characteristics of Indian culture *per se*.

Second, my definition of culture itself involves emotional interpretations, including not only cognitive maps and categories by which we interpret the world, but also physiological and emotional responses that contribute to the meaning(s) of an event. I have suggested elsewhere that interacting with people from different cultures involves developing what I have called cultural competencies, which in my definition include emotional congruence with an event. For example, suppose I am cognitively "aware" that Indian students generally speak in a closer physical space while interacting than Americans, and so, on a first encounter with an Indian, I sit closer. However, I feel uncomfortable while doing so, and interpret the event as unpleasant. Such behavior, based on cognitive awareness without emotional congruence, may occasion subsequent avoidance rather than continued interaction. Sharing feelings about an event over time, as in the case of doing an ethnography based on the bull's-eye question addressed here, can help people from different cultures to develop the cultural competencies in both cognitive and emotional terms in order to facilitate interaction.

A third reason for asking my informant how she felt about being a student here was more personal. At the time I initiated the project, I was in my first quarter at Stanford. I had just come to California after having lived outside the continental United States for over 10 years. I was not feeling at home at Stanford . . . in fact I wanted to know how another foreign student felt here. [I felt more foreign than American at that stage.] I think I was looking for a little support and perhaps some insights into my own personal dilemma. Along these same lines, choosing a topic which related to my personal dilemma would also serve as an example of how ethnography may be used to bring people together by underlining the commonalities in feelings and experiences.

In my attempts at finding out how my informant felt about being at Stanford, I found out a lot about American culture at Stanford and began to understand the culture shock I was myself experiencing at the time. Most importantly, I made a friend. In fact, we both made a friend.

The purpose of this chapter is to present the outcomes of our "ethnographic encounters" in the hope that others may learn a little more about their own culture and *feel* a little more about people from other cultures.

Procedure: the key informant approach

In conducting the ethnography, I interviewed one key informant. Finding my informant and establishing rapport came about quite naturally.

Why use one "key" informant?

Initially I had planned to interview three informants for about three hours each. But after the first three-hour interview, I was amazed at the value of going into depth with just one person. Three hours had passed, and we had just begun; I was just beginning to discover my own cultural myopia. So I decided to seek depth with one person instead of surveying the feelings of several. This also seemed the best way to achieve a means to develop empathy with someone from another culture. My aim was not to accurately and reliably describe Indian culture or the problems students from India generally experience at Stanford; I was seeking a means of learning to identify with another person's feelings, thereby breaking down cultural barriers.

Finding my key informant and establishing rapport

Finding my first informant, Mira, who became my key informant, came about quite naturally. Mira and I were participants in the same small discussion group. One day she happened to mention differences in the way American and Indian students respond in a classroom situation. I wondered what other observations and feelings Mira had about her experiences at Stanford and what things she had to adjust to. I asked if she would help me to understand what it felt like to be a graduate student here, from her perspective. Happily, she agreed.

Establishing rapport therefore came about easily. However, until that day, there had been very little interaction between us. We met in the lounge for the first and second interviews, and by the third, we had taken to the sun and the grass together. Nine hours of intensive discussions later, this is what resulted.

Cultural information which emerged

I began by finding out about Mira's background; then I asked the "grand tour" question and followed it where it led. A lot of information about American culture, as well as the culture of India, emerged through the principle of contrast as Mira expressed her thoughts and feelings about being here.

Mira's background

Mira was a female, married, graduate student from India. At Stanford she was in her first year of studies toward the M.A. in English. She belonged to what she termed, a "social elite", based on education and socio-economic status. Her husband was also a graduate student. We shall discuss the importance of "social class" in a later section.

My first insight into the simple nature of some cultural misunderstandings occurred when I asked, "Where are you from in India?" Mira responded that she was from the Punjab, so I *assumed* this to mean either that she was born in the Punjab, or that she lived there. Through subsequent listening I learned that she neither lived there nor was born there; the Punjab is where her parents were born. Although she was not born there and had never lived there, she considered herself a Punjabi.

> I'm from the Punjab . . . but I've never lived there.
> That's my native state. That's where my parents were born.
> I wasn't born there. It's a linguistic differentiation.
> I'm a Punjabi . . .

In this first few minutes of the first interview, I got my first insight into my own cultural bias: the assumption that regional identity depends on where one lives or was born. As an American, I identified first with things pertaining to my own existence; Mira, as an Indian, identified with things pertaining to her family and her family dialect. As Spradley and McCurdy (1972) state:

The ethnographer consciously seeks to be more objective . . . To be objective means to state the characteristics of objects and events as they exist and not to interpret, evaluate and prejudge them.

Suddenly these words took on meaning. I realized the conscious effort it would take to become objective; I did not *automatically* behave or listen that way, as I had assumed.

Asking the "grand tour" question

From this first experience of my own "loaded" listening, I realized how much my own questions would slant what I found out. How could I know what was important to Mira? All the questions I had planned to ask were really exemplary of my own cultural categories, not necessarily hers. I wanted somehow to know how Mira felt, how she categorized her experience at Stanford. In other words, I wanted an emic point of view.

Cultural behavior should always be studied and categorized in terms of the "inside view"—the "actors" definition of human events. That is, the units of conceptualization in anthropological theories should be "discovered" by analyzing the cognitive processes of the people studied, rather than "imposed" from cross-cultural classifications of behavior (Pelto, 1970: 68).

So instead of asking questions that would impose my own categories of comparison, (e.g. How do you like your classes? Do you think your relationship with professors is personal?), I simply began with one broad "grand tour" question and followed it where it led.

The purpose of grand tour questions is to obtain a preliminary survey of the meaning system your informant is using as well as to acquire many different category labels (Spradley and McCurdy, 1972: 63).

The question was simply, "How does it feel to be at Stanford?" I kept probing Mira's responses, deeper and deeper until we had exhausted the topic or Mira or both of us!

American culture at Stanford and the culture of India: learning through contrast

Combining emic and etic perspectives

A vivid picture of American culture was painted as Mira described how she felt at Stanford and discussed the things to which she had to adjust. Some of these were good, others bad, from her perspective. While American culture was clearly in the foreground, a picture of Indian culture also emerged, by contrast. After all, she was filtering and contrasting her experience in Stanford with her own system of meaning.

As Mira responded, several areas of her experience, several domains into which *she* categorized her experience at Stanford, emerged. These were, for example: the way Americans structure time; definitions of friendship; the concept of learning and approach to education; differences in values, such as the role of the individual with respect to the group; and the importance of family. I realized that these general domains could be compared across most cultures: most cultures structure time and transmit learning in particular ways, and most emphasize a particular position of the individual with respect to the group. Perhaps some of these general domains help underline what people have in common. The differences emerge in the particular attributes which give meaning to each domain, and the hierarchy of the domains themselves. For example, most cultures have some concept of family, but exactly who this includes, and the meaning attributed to particular kinship relationships, may differ.

While emic studies, through componential or other semantic analysis often provide significant guides to realistic "native" definitions of units of observation, these must be fitted to the researcher's cross-cultural (etic) concepts in order to test general propositions about human behaviour (Pelto, 1970: 86).

Through the principle of contrast, the ethnographic interviews with Mira often led to such *etic* comparisons of some general domains in the cultures of India and the United States. However, the domains were defined *emically*, i.e. according to the attributes which gave meaning to Mira's life.

Mira's thoughts and feelings

Mira seemed to enjoy many aspects of her experience at Stanford. She liked being exposed to new ideas, learning to think logically, and living in such a stimulating environment that offered so many things to do. However, these same factors—the abundance of things to do, the need for choice, the emphasis on critical thinking— also posed problems of adjustment and often created feelings of anxiety and/or fragmentariness. This last was a recurrent theme: Mira spoke of it in relation to the abundance of choice and the way Americans structure time, as exemplified by the quarter system, which had a fragmenting effect on friendship and learning. She kept mentioning a desire for "completeness". Mira felt also that the emphasis on critical analysis continually "poked holes" into ideas, to the detriment of learning. The intense pace of society, the abundance of things to do, the value given to extensiveness over intensity, the emphasis on and indulgence of the individual, with the resulting lack of group commitment, all contributed to her feeling of incompleteness. However, she rarely concluded with any overt criticism of American values, and always tried to reconcile the differences.

Mira's perspective on the cultures of America and India were expressed *explicitly*, through overt statements of her thoughts and feelings, as well as *implicitly*, through the ways in which she expressed herself, her body movements, the paralinguistic features of her speech, and the way she structured her arguments. I was amazed to see how her specific opinions and criticisms, as well as her form of expression, seemed congruent with her holistic perspective, which emphasized the complimentary nature of all aspects of life. She seemed to view the world as an integrated whole. Her form of expression reflected an integration of mind, body and emotion at every moment: while she was logically analyzing, she was waving her hands, staring with wide eyes into mine, and expressing her emotion through interjections, stress on particular words and changes in volume. She did not make the dichotomy of "now we think" and "now we feel" that marks American discourse.

For most of the remainder of this section, I shall present Mira's feelings about her experiences at Stanford in her own words—certainly a more accurate presentation than my paraphrasing and interpretation. The excerpts in each subsection are taken from the taped transcripts of our discussion, though I have 1) re-arranged and put together various excerpts which seem to address the same issue; 2) provided an operational label which seemed to characterize the general domain or issue addressed; and 3) introduced and/or commented on various excerpts, in order to draw attention to specific points.

What follows is an account of the cultural insights gained about both the culture of the United States (at Stanford) and the culture of India. As to the picture I saw of the American culture, I am left with the words of Robert Burns:

> Oh wad some power the giftie gie us
> To see oursels as others see us!

A note on typographical techniques used in the transcription:

Quotations	I am quoting from the tapes. All quotes are Mira's words unless a dialogue between us is marked: G = my words (usually questions) M = Mira's comments/responses
Four dots	within a quote: indicates I am quoting, but I have rearranged the order, (i.e. I have done a "cut and pasting" of comments that seem to fit together).

Parentheses ( )   within a quote: indicates I am including a word that was implied by the context in order to clarify passage.

Brackets [ ]   within or immediately following an excerpt: indicates that the bracketed words are my comment or interpretation—NOT part of the quote. I may say [Notice this or that].

Bold type   within a quote: indicates Mira's stress and/or increased volume on a particular word.

Italics   within a quote: indicates calling attention to implicit forms of expression, such as use of an interjection, e.g. *Ah!*; emotive language, e.g. *Oh my G-d!*) or words which avoid direct criticism, e.g. *perhaps, maybe*).

The quarter system and its effects

G: "How does it feel to be a graduate student in America?

M: It's a difficult question to answer. The educational situation is different. It's structured differently—completely. It's not by this quarter system."

Effects on friendship

M: In India (students take) a set course that's offered. One of the results of this is on a graduate or undergraduate level; you are with the same group of students for that entire period, **through every class.**

G: Do you think it's good to be with the same group of students?

M: Certainly, if you consider that social interaction is an important part of learning, or that you can learn a lot from other students, and that friendship matters. I only realize the importance of this to me since I've been here.

G: Do you think that social interaction matters much here at Stanford?

M: Education is structured in a way that that isn't forward. If it's important, then the individual has to seek it for himself. [Notice how she avoids criticizing directly.] It's quite likely that if students here are taking a number of courses, you don't meet the same people. Even if you did, next quarter you wouldn't, so it's not a prolonged acquaintance.

In India in my studies, the 2 years I studied, I met the same group of people for 2 years in every class, so the type of relationship you build up is the type that never exists here.

G: Have you made friends with any of the American students?

M: I've made acquaintances, but not friends.

G: How do you distinguish the two?

M: The amount of interaction. In the Indian situation there's bound to be more because of the time you are together in the same classes. This is a more superficial relationship. It's entirely superficial.

G: How do you define superficial?

M: It's the depth that exists. I have interesting conversations with people for fifteen minutes which may proceed in depth in only one fragmented aspect—it doesn't go beyond that . . so my relationships with people exist in this entirely fragmented way . . . .

I talk to someone for half an hour and we talk about her problems or we talk about what we've been doing, but that might be the only time we talk for three months or six months, during which time it's not necessary to contact that person. With my **friends** it's different. I have a lot of acquaintances whom I don't really value very much . . It's a fragmentary communication . . . . I don't have a total communication with anybody.

The notion of superficiality or fragmentariness in personal encounters was a recurrent theme, which Mira felt was also expressed in language conventions:

M: One of the things that really disturbed me when I first got here, because I just couldn't react to it, is that people are overtly very friendly, to strangers that walk past you—if you happen to meet their eyes—they acknowledge it. They say, "How are you doing?" and for me that's the weirdest question to ask a stranger because it's a question that demands an extended reply. And you don't give an extended reply to a stranger. So when somebody asked, "How are you doing?" I was completely flummered. So what do I say? Do I start from the beginning? Do I give my entire history? How am I supposed to react to this statement?

   What is so funny is that people say it and then they rush on. They don't expect an answer necessarily other than a smile or a nod. So that's interesting. And sometimes if you start off on an extended answer to someone who asks this question, they are very uncomfortable because they didn't intend to get into this conversation anyway . . . .

   When people ask you to talk about yourself, I guess I felt that that person was not really interested in listening . . . .

G: Were you ever disillusioned, disappointed, that in instances in which the overt social behavior seemed at first very friendly, you then found that it wasn't continued.

M: Yes. *Sometimes.* Definitely because they make overtures that to me are extremely **personal** overtures. To ask somebody, "How are you doing?" is a personal question. Yes, it does make you feel uncomfortable. You don't want to **bore** the other person—to take up his or her time. You want to give him the kind of cultural response that he expects.

Mira was always quick to qualify any statement which would be interpreted as a criticism of American culture. She usually ended by indicating that the root of the problem was not in American culture, but rather in *her*, be it in her lack of knowledge, her personality, or her background. (I shall point this out from time to time as it occurs throughout her comments.) For example, in a later point in the above conversation, she mentioned that she now understood the cultural context of this greeting:

M: They were just sort of making a friendly acquaintance. "Yes, I see you. You're a human being. Yes, you saw me. I'm acknowledging it." . . . .

   I felt that I over-react to that statement. I have to learn not to over-react so much, because people don't expect it. It's not the right kind of cultural response.

Similarly, Mira pointed out various problems of interaction due to her lack of knowledge of "what is culturally appropriate to say" and "what cultural assumptions are implied" in particular situations. (Erickson, Hymes and Cazden would call these "differences in communicative etiquette". Gumperz would call these "differences in sociolinguistic conventions in speaking" and "different cultural assumptions" about the particular situation.)

M: What particularly inhibits my own degree of interaction with others is because I don't say the same things.

G: What do you mean?

M: In anything to do with the way people react to each other's behaviors—their problems. For instance, when I watch TV I'm constantly saying only an American could make a joke like that. That is something that is foreign.

Effects on learning

Learning alone vs learning from others

M: The reason why it's different over here is that everybody is much more isolated in terms of the work they're doing, the courses of study they're taking. In India in an undergraduate or graduate program, you're one person **within** a group. That makes a big difference. Over here to have that kind of relationship would take a lot of effort because the structure is against it. . . .

(Over here) they just don't have time for a lot of other things.

G: Why do people have so little time here?

M: They want to make the most out of education.

G: In India, don't they want to make the most out of education?

M: Certainly, but in India we do that **with** people. . . .

I don't separate the "learning" from "learning **through** people" who are around me. I learned more through my friends—as much as I did from books or from teachers or courses, so that is a **complete** experience.

In a later conversation she reiterated the same point:

M: I realize how much I learn through the people I know rather than merely through books, because for me an idea or body of knowledge becomes interesting only when there is a human mind that grapples with it. So when you have two or three people who discuss, whatever it is comes alive and it's much more interesting and it's sort of deepened by that, so I value that because that is education . . . .

G: Is there something you're feeling inadequate about here?

M: Anxiety about achievement in academic terms. It's more important for me to feel that I have personally **learned** something—have grown—whether or not I get the grades is not as important, yet grades are important because you need some external confirmation of your own success.

Effects on intellectual growth

G: Are you happy with the quarter system?

M: For some courses, yes, because three months is enough, but for others I feel I'm just beginning to get into something, and the quarter ends. It takes longer to grasp a concept. *Maybe* it's the way I am. (The advantage is that) you don't *flog a subject to death*, which you sometimes do in India. You don't have that kind of pressure that you do in India. (Also) you don't have this quarter system—the amount you're supposed to remember in India can be a burden—basically a hindrance to any kind of growth. [Notice her careful qualifications here.]

G: Do you think that the quarter system relates to the fragmentary environment?

M: *Perhaps*—it doesn't give me this feeling of completeness that I want. [Notice her value of "completeness" stated here.]

Sometimes I think that's also because of my particular background. There is a lot that is unknown or disconnected, but *maybe* if you've done a lot of courses in this area it's less likely that you have this feeling.
[Notice again her qualification and avoidance of direct criticism of the quarter system.]

Education: Mira's holistic approach vs the scientific method

A holistic approach and desire for "completeness"

Mira wanted to see the "whole" picture. For Mira, education meant development, and that meant completeness:

G: What kinds of things is education about?

M: About anything—a course, an idea, film, personal development, growth, problems that I have, relationships, hopes—

G: What kind of hopes?

M: that I will leave this experience with some kind of sense of **completeness**—that I have finished with this . . this lovely feeling of coherence, conceptual clarity.

Again Mira mentions her desire for a feeling of completeness in contrast to the fragmentariness she has experienced at Stanford.

On absolutes and the need to qualify

All of Mira's comments were marked by a tendency to qualify statements and a desire to reconcile opposing points of view. She never ended a comment with a direct criticism. Indeed, she herself qualified almost every criticism she made. For Mira, everything had advantages and disadvantages, and what could be termed "opposing" or "contradictory" positions were for her, complementary. For Mira, there were no absolutes and hence, no mutually exclusive points of view.

M: If someone makes a statement and I know that that can not be an absolute statement, I probably qualify it in my mind. It could be a product of culture. I'm not a religious person, but the Hindu religion is one that encourages multifaceted approaches to things. It's a religion that more than most religions embraces contradictions. [Then she even qualifies her point about Hinduism:] There is a separation between Hindu philosophy and its practice. Practicing can be very narrow. Qualification is a product of personal growth.

On specialization

From Mira's perspective, education at Stanford was somewhat absolutist. She viewed absolutism as a function of overspecialization. She felt that ideas tended to be analyzed and evaluated in terms of a single theory or point of view to the exclusion of others:

M: The only thing I'm resisting is I'm aware that it's an entire academic system, especially in the social sciences, that I'm being immersed in and that certain types of analysis or ways of looking at things are perceived as the right way—a specific cultural peculiarity in academics here.. It is not clear, but I'm beginning to learn that in papers, if I analyze it in a certain way, whoever's reading it likes a certain type. I haven't exactly formed in my mind what are the criteria, but I know if I say things that have been proved in experiments elsewhere, the findings in the behavioral sciences that are applied vaguely to the way I'm going to analyze the problem, it is appreciated, and that is what is seen as being intelligent or valid....

    I don't know—I also feel here, which I didn't in India, that teachers in India are not so specialized. Over here it is likely that a different teacher has—a specific axe to grind—and then you present things to him from that point of view, and he'll present things to you from that point of view. For instance, when you study literature—that's one subject that's capable of a *tremendous* variety of interpretations—shading, if you persist in looking at models, or only from one point of view, say the psycho-sexual point of view, then you are coloring the whole analysis.

G: And you think we do that here?

M: We have a lot of people who have done research in an area and they have become **specialized** and very interested in that area, so obviously it becomes overtly loaded on one particular angle or dimension—many people with *tremendous* reputations, who have written books, but are basically not very good teachers.

G: In India do they seem to take one point of view like that?

M: I don't think the majority would. There's a difference in the fact that you have to do research, and doing research here **means** limiting—taking a specialized viewpoint. When you go into such depth into one aspect, which is essentially what you have to do in research, it colors your whole vision. You lose out on a broader sense of things.

G: Which of the two is more important: the general or the specialized?

M: *Sometimes* the specialized gives you a lot of *tremendous* insights, and it helps. All the specialized results put together give you an advance in your critical thinking about something, but when that kind of a person teaches, he teaches only from one standpoint. It can be unsettling to those who are learning. You feel that you're **blinkered** in some sense—that this is not the only way of seeing it!

G: Does that make you feel uncomfortable?

M: Good in a way, because it stimulates you to think, "How valid is what is being said? how comprehensive? why does he pick out these things?" It's good if it makes you do these things. [Notice all these qualifications and avoidance, again, of directly criticizing, but her feelings emerge as we continue:]

G: Do you feel comfortable with it?

M: I **feel** very uncomfortable with it.

Over-emphasis on critical analyses at Stanford: "poking holes"

M: (Here) there is a tremendous emphasis on criticizing something—never accepting anything at face value. (The) emphasis is on being critical rather than receptive. . . .

I do believe it's important that you learn to think and learning to think involves being critical, but I don't think it's valuable to emphasize so much that we must be critical—we must **destroy.** [More qualifications . .]

When people pick out contradictions—I did a course on Nietsche—the fact that a person is contradictory doesn't mean everything falls apart. You may admit that, "yes, there are these contradictions," but consider the value of the idea for itself! *Perhaps* things can exist in contradiction without falling into nothing, so if you're really quick to criticize inconsistency in form, *sometimes* I feel *perhaps* you missed the main thing. "What is the value of what he is saying?" . . . .

It can be very destructive because it's a way of looking at things (in which you) shut your mind to what is valuable in it. You just aren't **receptive** anymore. When you're presented with a study or a finding, you must pick holes because that's what you've been trained to do. You pick holes immediately. I think what is of greater value is *perhaps* that you evaluate it constructively first, and whatever holes you pick, don't make a big thing out of it.

It's as if the whole study or findings have collapsed just because you've picked two small holes. All you try to do is see what's wrong with it—which is in some sense *maybe* the wrong perspective. What is more important: the few holes that you've picked, or the overall emphasis of the study?

Mira points out that education in India presents the opposite extreme:

G: Did you notice this in India?

M: In India criticism is something that is just absent. It's the other extreme. You are sort of like a *sponge.*

That's not a fundamental aspect of Indian culture, that you learn to be critical. On the other hand, you learn subservience, obedience. . . . criticism is important because you have in some way proved that you have assimilated it—that you're thinking about it—that you're not a passive recipient of the learning process—*not a sponge or lump* which takes in everything. That's why it's valued.

M: But they can put pressure on someone and that can lead people to make *idiotic* criticism just for the sake of making criticisms. [She vacillates here, not wanting to end her point on a critical note:] It's a question of the way you've been trained—not just to take in things without reflecting on them. It's a way of thinking about things, of learning, so it **is** valuable.

      My background has neglected this. I feel *angry* that my education is
something that I had to achieve myself. They didn't teach you to think
logically—the assumptions behind things. . . .

G: Do you think that criticizing discrete points relates to that fragmentary thing
again?

M: *Sometimes* I think this reaction on my part is a defensive reaction, because
perhaps I have not been trained. It's not the way my mind works. I can't pick
holes as quickly as the way it's demanded here. It's not an easy thing for me;
(others) **jump** at things that are wrong. *Perhaps* I'm not clever enough.

Notice how she qualifies her criticism again, never ending with a criticism of
American culture or schooling at Stanford. For Mira, there are advantages and
disadvantages to both critical analysis and receptivity, which in the extreme she calls
"subservience and obedience". Again, the two positions are not mutually exclusive,
but complementary, reflecting her holistic perspective. Through these excerpts, her
own "logical" analyses is complementarily marked by descriptive and emotive
language. In these excerpts we also again see Mira's desire to put the responsibility on
herself, e.g. "perhaps I'm not clever enough". But no opinion, even ones in which she
is the object of criticism, is definite. We see a constant use of "sometimes" and
"perhaps" in her comments.

Dangers of growing up in America: value differences

At one point in the interviews I asked Mira if she would like to stay in America and
raise children here. She felt it would be difficult because of differences in values:

M: That's one of the things that would disturb me the most about settling down
    here. I already have some system of values.

Mira's own values emerged by contrast as she discussed the American values she
perceived as somewhat conflicting with her own. In this regard, she discussed the *pace*
of society, the *abundance and variety* of things to do and buy, and the role of *choice*,
individualism, *materialism* and *commitment*.

Pace, variety and choice

Mira observed an intense pace in American society which she related to the variety
of things to do. Like everything Mira mentioned, these had both advantages and
disadvantages. On the one hand, the pace was lively and the environment filled with
desirable things to do. On the other hand, the pace reflected a greater value in
"variety" and "extensity" than in "quality" and "intensity" according to Mira. She
also experienced tremendous anxiety in trying to choose among so many options.

Pace and variety

M: The pace of life is **much** more intense here. At this university itself—the
    amount of things that happen. There is nobody rushing around in India. In
    India there is very little to do—drives me mad. [Notice emotive language
    again.] . . . .

One of the things that's most enriching about this place is the amount of things to do.

While it would seem from the above comment that Mira liked the pace, because the lack of things to do in India "drove her mad", the slow pace in India was an advantage in establishing friendships and in developing the sense of completeness and control that she wanted for her life:

M: Here each person is rushing out, doing whatever it is. In India you share a lot of things together.

G: What kind of things?

M: Maybe not dramatic things—you may just sit and talk.... You don't interact so much and then break it up. You don't open up your soul to someone for five minutes and the next second you're back where you started.

G: Could it also be a function that on certain levels American society moves much quicker and then it stops abruptly? [I hope I didn't put words into her mouth. I was trying to summarize from her previous comments and see if I got the meaning she intended to imply.]

M: Definitely. That's the best way to say it.

She then continued to qualify:

M: It depends on what you're like as a person—if you're content, if you seek intense experience, if you want more quality in your experiences than just variety, then you'll be content with a close circle of friends who you get to know better and better. My parents are that way. They have a close circle of friends. They meet constantly with the same people over again, and they don't enjoy large gatherings with fragmentary interactions. I guess it differs from people to people.

Choice and anxiety

M: In my first quarter I went *berserk* because I was like a child who was going to get ice cream for the first week and no longer after that. I started feeling I have to do this and that.. One of my closest friends *went nuts*. She just would not stop. She wants to embrace all of life in one go.. Unless you have the discipline to say, "I will not submit to that—I cannot live at that pace.."

G: Has that been an adjustment problem?

M: I had the impression that every minute of your timetable was full and I knew when I live like that I don't feel my life is *full*. I just feel that I've lost control of it. [Notice her desire for completeness expressed again by "full".]....

G: Do you think that Americans are "stuffing their lives"?

M: I don't think people here are pressurized. Foreigners might be more pressurized because they don't get this kind of cultural experience. I don't think Americans go berserk because there are three films on and a recital as well. Most of the students here are pretty accustomed to their academic work. That would only be a problem for a foreign student and only one who wasn't being paid by his government to study like a *maniac* and would not have time to look right or left. [Continually very descriptive and emotive in her accounts.]....

G: What are the bad things in the concept of choice itself?

M: For a student who is new (to it) it can lead to a lot of anxiety because you don't know what to do. If you come from a system where you're not accustomed to making decisions, it can cause a lot of anxiety because you don't know if you're making the best choices and you are generally at a loss.

G: Have you felt this (anxiety)?

M: Yes, very acutely—very acutely. I both enjoyed the fact there is a choice and resented it extremely because it caused so many problems.

G: What other kinds of problems?

M: Well, they arise from the structured education I come from. We don't select courses; you have much less choice. Suppose I wanted to do a Master's in Literature (in India). There wouldn't be a range of courses which I choose from. A Master's in Literature means I have to do whatever is offered. I may have a choice in relation to what I choose for a minor but there is very little elective choice. . . .

   If you put someone who's had a very structured education into an unstructured situation, then you face the problem that you don't really know what you want to choose because you've not been told what to do. It happens every time I have to write a paper: I never know what to write it on. I have a **tremendous** problem trying to decide what I should write on—which stems from years of education in which we had no real choice. . You've been guided very heavily.

Individualism, materialism and lack of commitment

Mira viewed the abundance of things to do, the pace of society and the need for choice as related to the American emphasis on individualism, materialism and lack of commitment.

Individualism: pros and cons

M: (Here there is) the necessity for you to define yourself basically. The onus is on you in a way that it is not in India.

While Mira enjoyed many aspects of individualism, one of the reasons she wouldn't want to bring up a child here was because of what she viewed as over-indulgence of individualism.

Pros

M: Individuality is not a value in India like it is over here.

G: Which would be the greater value (in India)?

M: Conformity is—to do whatever is acceptable or whatever is demanded. Generally speaking, "doing your own thing" is something basically alien to Indian culture.

G: How do you feel about it?

M: I enjoy it in a way because there is possibly less anxiety here than in India, because I am in an alien environment. There aren't many expectations. (There is) intense anxiety at home, because of what people expect from you. It's the most enslaving thing: other people's expectations. . . .

(In India there are) a lot of social constraints which are very hampering in your relationships.

G: What kind of social constraints?

M: For instance, for a girl—*endless* constraints—what you can do, what you can not do, whom you can be seen with, how long, and when you can do it.

G: What do you mean? In sexual terms?

M: *Oh* yes, totally—in terms of ordinary social intercourse with the other sex—it's limited.

M: Even at university in India?

M: Yes. As an undergraduate my parents allowed me to go to only so many parties and insisted that I came back at a certain time—very strict constraints . .

In another example Mira mentioned fewer constraints in the American manner of dress:

M: One has the freedom to be sloppy, at least occasionally—that I value here.

G: What do you mean, "sloppy"?

M: For instance, if you have a get together or party, everybody doesn't dress up *like crazy* like they do in India. I don't like that too much. I enjoy the comfort that you don't **have to** dress up all the time.

Cons

G: Would you like a child to grow up in this system?

M: In India I would be able to check the influences because I know the environment so well. On the other hand, here they don't have to be submissive or docile as in India. At the same time what I really fear here is the kind of almost total indulgence of the child. [Notice all these qualifications. She does not directly answer "no" but it is implied.]

G: What do you mean?

M: Indulgence of individualism in general.

Materialism

M: A child in this society would almost be a victim of the prevailing values.

G: What would a child be victim of?

M: Materialism—of the amount of things you have in this place. It's not easy for a child to walk into a shop which is teeming with things and say, "Well, I don't want them—this is not really necessary." I consider that a problem. I don't want a child who is in a society that creates that kind of thing. That to me is really serious. It's a consumer society. India is also, but to a lesser degree, so they are more free in India—not pressurized by so many things.

G: What other values would a child be victim of?

M: Am I going to get a job that is going to make me work *like a donkey* but will make me a lot of money—but will cut off everything else? Am I going to dance the tune, run along with the rat race: How far can I compromise on that? [Notice her emotional and vivid descriptions, and use of metaphors.]

G: Do you think "working your guts out for money" is more an American value?

M: Here you have to if you want to rise. You generally have to slog. [Without directly saying, "yes", she again tries to justify or explain it, but "yes" is implied. Her continual way of making this kind of response, indirectly, expresses another cultural attribute: one of courteousness and less "confrontation".]

G: What do you mean, "slog"?

M: Aggressiveness seems to be something you need to survive in this place. You need to be able to push. Those things are valued—to have drive, to impose yourself on reality. Otherwise you won't get anywhere. Everybody will walk over you.

G: In India you don't have to push?

M: That's because in India I come from a class that has a silver spoon in their mouths. [Notice her mention of "class". I focus on this topic later].

Commitment

At one point I asked Mira what values she would like her own children to have. It was a hypothetical question because she did not have any children. Her response indicated her own value of commitment while it also reflected her opinion that Americans lacked commitment. She felt this lesser sense of commitment was influenced by the amount of choices available.

M: If they were getting married, it's important that they didn't view it as a kind of experiment. Marriage is something that works if you are determined it has to work, and if you have a basic commitment to it—not if you have the basic feeling that you can always get out of it because then you're less likely to work at it, *perhaps*.

G: Do you think that lack of commitment is characteristic of Americans?

M: It's because you have so much choice. You have other alternatives, and look at the divorce rate. I may be generalizing *wildly* but I'm not saying you have perfect marriages (in India.) You have *hellish* conditions which you live with. But you don't have this kind of divorce rate—and I think that marriages are happier in India, simply because there are not so many choices. [Notice again the emotive and descriptive language.]

Mira also viewed lack of commitment as a function of the mobility that exists here:

M: (Here) you can move in different circles. People are very mobile. They're in one place for one year and somewhere else for another. . . .

If society is so structured that a person is meeting other people, it's all right to meet other people and interact with other people outside of marriage, how can you help but not have situations when you get involved with other people, outside?

G: Let's take that analogy to the situation of two friends. You mentioned earlier that you like to have one or two close friends and here the situation is very fragmented. Could that be an analogous situation in that you don't make a commitment to one friend?

M: Perhaps.

Life in India

While most of the discussion emphasized Mira's feelings about life in America, a part of the discussion focused on what life was like for her in India. Even when this was not the direct focus, I learned a lot about Indian society by contrast. In this brief section I include the gist of what she expressed and what she missed most about being away from India, family life and social classes.

What Mira missed about being here

G: What kinds of things do you miss?

   Ah! Oh G-d! I miss my family, my parents, I miss music, I miss dance .. I miss a lot of things. [Notice the "paralinguistic" as well as direct expressions of emotion here.]

Music and Dance

G: You don't think there's dance here?

M: I miss **Indian** music, **Indian** dance.

G: What is it about Indian music that attracts you?

M: Well, I **studied** it—Indian classical vocal music—for a while. It's one of the things I *tremendously regret* being here—because I can't continue that, and I'm very interested in it.

   [Notice how she was attracted to what she had a personal investment in. This is a point I will return to in the last section.]

Family closeness

While Mira mentioned a variety of things she missed, the close interaction with her family was clearly in the foreground:

G: And you mentioned you miss your family.

M: Oh yes, I miss my family **terribly.**

G: Do you have a large family?

M: No, I have one brother and one sister.

G: Were you very close?

M: Pretty close—I don't know. I guess we're close. I'm very close with my parents.

G: What does "close" mean?

M: Uh—it means I basically **share** a lot with them, and it's interesting that I am much closer to them now, being married and being away, than I was as an adolescent; I went through this period of estrangement—which I think most adolescents do—and this period of feeling that the gulf between us was immense, but now I know that that's not true really. I don't know. I am pretty close to my sister and my brother, and getting more and more close as we grow older and the gap lessens.

G: Do you feel American family life is the same as in India?

M: *Maybe* it's different *in a way*; maybe it differs from family to family; [Notice all the "indefinite" markers and the qualifications.] There is certainly a more "each person doing his own thing", even in the family.

G: Here?

M: Yes—I feel—*perhaps* more of it than in India. We share a lot (in India), but I think there are families here which do certainly share a lot and are pretty close. It's something that's partly individual. [More qualifications!]

G: Would you and your family spend a lot of time with your family in India?

M: *Ah! Oh my G-d!* A **lot** of time! My husband is very much, even closer to his family than I am.

G: "A lot of time"—what does that mean? How often would you go over to see them?

M: Now we live separately. That's a very big thing in India . . We lived in Bombay and both our parents, his parents and my parents, live in Bombay, but we didn't live with them. We lived alone, separately. That's not normal. It would be normal if you didn't live in the same town.

G: But in the same town you'd normally live with them?

M: Sometimes you *might*. There was a lot of pressure on me to live with my in-laws, which I resisted *madly*. But certainly I met my parents twice a week and we didn't have a phone. If we'd had a phone, I might have met them less, because I'd talk to them more on the phone. So I made up for it by going there a lot, and I miss that. Because even though I was teaching in India, I had a house to run and I didn't have *a battalion of servants* or whatever—I didn't keep that kind of thing—but I still always had this basic insecurity. My mother was there and I could go talk to her. My sister was there. Very often I went, I mean we met very often . . and with my in-laws, it was equally so—at least twice a week if not more. [Notice the continuity of seeing the same family members in contrast to the lack of continuity in her relationships with people at Stanford. Against this background, the "fragmentariness" she perceives around her is understandably heightened.]

G: When you had social activities in India, did you spend a lot of time with family or with other people?

M: Well, it's kind of even—at least as much time with the family as with peers.

In the above excerpt, notice how "servants" were interjected into a discussion that focused not on social class or servants but on the amount of time family members spend together, and the custom that young married couples usually live with their families.

Social classes and the role of servants

The notion of social class itself was a recurrent theme expressed both directly and indirectly throughout the discussions. Class seemed to be more important in India than America. However, Mira's conception of class was based more on socio-economic status than the caste one was born into. I did not expect this response, so you will notice how I kept questioning her on this point:

G: You mentioned something about your social class earlier.

M: Very, very upper class—infinitesimal proportion of the population, socio-economic, education and all the rest.

G: It's not based so much on caste now?

M: Once you reach a certain socio-economic status, and you go to certain schools and colleges, then this loses importance.

G: It's not important how you get it? How do they get it? What is it based on?

M: It's based on the standing of their parents—if you come from a high socio-economic family.

G: How do **they** get money? It's not caste-related?

M: Not necessarily, but to a degree it is. I probably belong to Chatriya caste—the caste that in my area was administrative, the warriors, professional people. The Brahmins are the intellectuals, the religious. Then you have others—e.g. the Vaisya: those in business, the merchant class. I think I come from this caste (Chatriya). I'm not very sure. It's something that's been lost.

G: Has the caste system been lost?

M: Not in India today, but in my family. In most people of this particular socio-economic status, it has been lost. Caste is not so important anymore. For instance, when I was married, my parents were not bothered about a particular class, but a lower level, the middle level, still cares.

G: But did your parents care that your husband was from the same social class as you?

M: I don't think they cared.

G: But is he?

M: He is. He is from exactly the same class, the same state, the same socio-economic background. I don't think they would care, only in the sense if he was from a completely different background—in terms of social class—they would have worried about adjustment problems. If he was economically insufficient, they would have worried about that. After all, parents do worry how you're going to take care of yourselves.

Several other times during our discussions, Mira indicated that people of her class had "a silver spoon in their mouths". Having servants seemed also to be important. While she mentioned several times that she didn't have "that sort of thing", having or not having servants was nevertheless mentioned in several different contexts. For example, I asked Mira what kinds of things she had to adjust to, how she had to modify her life, to cope in America. She replied:

M: Very few things.... (However) for a person *of my class* who comes to this country I guess one of the major adjustments to be made would be adjusting to doing physical work at home, because girls *from my class* don't cook, they don't clean house, they don't wash clothes. That would be a major adjustment. But I didn't find that because I didn't have *so many servants*. That wasn't a big shift for me, but that could be *for someone of my class*.

Mira was doing housework while at Stanford. She made similar comments when I asked her how she felt about it:

G: About cleaning someone else's house—how do you feel?

M: I don't have those hangups, which is peculiar *for a member of my class*. It would be unthinkable in India. I chose to do it voluntarily. I wanted a job that wouldn't make me sit. That wouldn't involve reading—that was mindless.

This section on "life in India" is rather brief in relation to sections which focused on Mira's reactions to America. The reasons for this are twofold: the goal of this mini-ethnography was not to describe Indian culture, but rather to get to know Mira—how she felt about being in America; and my own personal dilemma prompted me to want to learn more about American culture from the perspective of a foreign student. Our discussions certainly did provide me with insights about this and about the bases for the "culture shock" I myself was experiencing.

My interpretation of Mira's thoughts and feelings: a summary

Mira's thoughts and feelings about being at Stanford seemed to form a pattern, marked by an array of fragmentary, disconnected elements. The pace was fast, stimuli were abundant, and personal experience was extensive. Personal development seemed to be defined in terms of individual academic achievement. People learned to think critically, precisely. It is as if life were a fascinating series of clear, precise snapshots or single frames in which the individual was the star. However, put them together and there was little continuity. As a motion picture it was inadequate if not absurd.

By contrast, Mira's own values for completeness and her holistic perspective emerged, in which differing elements were not mutually exclusive nor opposing, but rather complementary parts of an integrated whole. Mira's linguistic expression was marked by careful qualifications and frequent use of indefinite forms of agreement or disagreement. "Perhaps" and "sometimes" were more frequently heard than definite "yes" or "no". There were no blacks and whites used in this cultural painting, but rather shades of grey. The hues were not discrete, but rather continuous. From Mira's perspective, the focus was not on the single frame, but on the film in motion. The star of her film was not the individual, but "us". Personal development, learning and life itself took on meaning primarily in their relationship to others. Her concept of friendship symbolized her entire perspective:
"I define myself through my relationship with my friend."

Self-awareness and the making of a friendship

Know others and know thyself

"In many ways the saying 'Know thyself' is not well said.
It were more practical to say, 'Know other people'."
(Menander, *Thrasyleon,*
343–292 B.C.
translated by Francis C. Allison, in
Bartlett's *Famous
Quotations*, 196: 27b)

As I was working on this ethnography, I came to realize more and more that I, too, defined myself in my relationships with other people—people who I categorized as "significant other". By "significant" I mean people with whom I interact emotionally as well as cognitively, i.e. people who are at once catalysts and essential elements in the chemistry of my emotional and intellectual interpretations of the world. Through the interviews with Mira I came to realize that my loneliness at Stanford was because there were no "significant others" in my life here, and thus, the definition of "self" had come to a static halt. In this static state, I was feeling empty or even worse, almost as if something inside me were disintegrating—although I did not understand these feelings. The interviews with Mira uncovered several new keyholes in my understanding. One keyhole led to an initial grasp of the dynamic quality of life itself. In the absence of any dynamic interrelationships with significant others, I began to understand my negative emotions as well as what I considered to be my intellectual unproductivity.

Mira's account of American culture served to crystallize the culture shock which I myself was going through, but had not been aware of. But perhaps the most surprising keyhole I peeked through was the one that gave me a glimpse at my own behaviors. Like Mira, I observed people rushing around, doing a variety of things, engaged in intense but fragmentary relationships and endeavors. I, too, criticized these things and wondered if I should remain in America. But it was only through Mira's specific examples that I became aware that I was myself very much one of those people that I had been criticizing. I saw myself fragmented and running from place to place, course to course, person to person and feeling to feeling. I saw myself in the candy store, trying to grasp it all. I too had said, "How are you?" and continued walking before I heard the response. Through Mira's account I became aware that to a large extent, I was responsible for my negative feelings because I had unconsciously fallen into many of the cultural behaviors which I was negatively reacting to! This awareness not only provided me with an understanding of my culture shock, but more importantly, it gave me valuable insights as to how to constructively modify behaviors to develop dynamic relationships with significant others and to achieve the continuity of experience that I, like Mira, sought.

It became increasingly clear to me that learning to know someone else, to become sensitive to someone else's feelings, is not only an invaluable experience in its own right, but is also a remarkable exercise in self-awareness.

Learning to listen: confessions of a talker

Getting to know someone else involves creative listening. By creative listening I mean, like Textor (1978b), listening actively, with concentration to every detail, probing and encouraging informants to continually refine their thoughts on a given topic until the speaker's meanings are clear.

Through the interviews with Mira I was somewhat surprised at my new insights regarding aspects of Indian culture. In my undergraduate year in Spain, I had roomed with a lady from India, Eileen, whom I later visited in India. While we had become close friends, the interviews with Mira made me realize how little I must have learned about how Eileen thought and felt. My feeling about Eileen was that she was a great conversationalist. We spent hours "talking". Ten years later I now realize what an excellent listener Eileen was. Eileen may have learned a lot about my personal thoughts and feelings, the way I structure and interpret my world and as a result of the personal feelings I expressed as well as the continuity of our relationship, we did become friends, meaningful friends. But now—some 10 years later—after the ethnographic interviews with Mira, I realize how little I must have understood about what Eileen was thinking and feeling. I realize how much I assumed, and worst of all, how much I had talked! I realize that other people like to express what is important to them and to be listened to as much as I do! As I write these words, I am not only a little embarrassed by my lack of sensitivity to "other" but also rather sad at the opportunity I missed to really get to know Eileen. My only consolation is that the awareness of my own talkativeness and the experience of learning to listen creatively during this ethnography has helped me to learn more about, and from others ever since.

Taking the time to go into depth

I recently saw a contemporary card with the single phrase: "Things take time."

At first glance the phrase may appear trite, but now I realize the simple truth it conveys. It takes time to get to know someone else, to know how they structure and interpret the world, what is important to them, what causes them anxiety and fulfillment. It takes time to get past the readily perceived differences to the fundamental commonalities. It takes time to become friends. Doing this ethnography provided the setting for taking time to become friends, time which neither Mira nor I might otherwise have taken. Mira and I talked about this as we sat on the grass during our last interview:

G: "I feel sad today that the project is over. But I hope this is just the beginning of a friendship. If the course served to do that, to make the time to sit and to really talk to someone—

M: Few can do that here. I don't create time to sit on the grass.

G: And me, today, with a paper due tomorrow and an exam, I probably wouldn't have made the time to sit out here on the grass with you and learn more."

While that day marked the end of our formal meetings, it was the beginning of a friendship. Taking the time not only provides a means for getting to know someone else; the commitment of time and energy to someone or something makes that person or thing more meaningful. I remember the dialogue between the lion and the little prince in my favorite book:

"I can't play with you," said the lion. "I'm not tamed."

"What does 'tamed' mean?"

"It's something too forgotten," said the lion. "It means to believe in bonds. To you I'm only one lion, like a hundred thousand others. But if you tame me, we'll need each other. You will be, for me, unique to the world. I will be, for you, unique. One only knows the things he tames," said the lion. "People buy things ready made in stores. But since there are no stores that sell friends, man doesn't have friends anymore. If you want a friend, tame me!"

(Saint-Exupery, *Le Petit Prince*, 1946: 69: my translation)

References

Adler, P. (1976) Beyond cultural identity: reflections on cultural and multicultural man, in L. Samovar and R. Porter (eds.) *Intercultural Communication*, Belmont, Ca: Wadsworth Publishing Company.

Anderson, N. H. (1965) Averaging vs. adding as a stimulus-combination rule in impression formation, *Journal of Experimental Psychology*, **70**, 394–400.

Archer, D. and Akert, R. M. (1977) Words and everything else: verbal and nonverbal cues in social interpretation, *Journal of Personality and Social Psychology*, **35**, 443–49.

Aronson, E. (1972) *The Social Animal*, San Francisco: W. H. Freeman and Company.

Asher, J. (1969) The total physical response technique of learning, *Journal of Special Education No. 3,*, 253–262.

Badia, P., Culbertson, S. and Harch, J. (1973) Choice of longer or stronger signalled shock over shorter or weaker unsignalled shock, *Journal of the Experimental Analysis of Behavior*, **19** (1), 25–32.

Bandura, A. (1977) *Social Learning Theory*, New Jersey: Prentice Hall.

Bandura, A. (1978) Values and Objectives, Observational learning, Enactive learning, mimeographed chapters, on reserve, Stanford University, Main Library, November.

Banks, J. A. (1979) *Teaching Strategies for Ethnic Studies*, Boston: Allyn and Bacon, 2nd edition.

Barnett, H. (1960) *Being a Paluan*. CSCA. New York: Rinehard and Winston, Inc.

Bartlett, F. C. (1932) *Remembering*. London: Cambridge University Press.

Berlin, B. and Kay, P. (1969) *Basic Color Terms*. Berkeley: University of California Press.

Berger, J., Cohen, B. P. and Zelditch, M., Jr. (1966) Status characteristics and expectation states, in J. Berger, M. Zelditch, Jr. and B. Anderson (eds.), *Sociological Theories in Progress*. Boston: Houghton-Miffin.

Berreman, G. (1972) Is ethnoscience relevant? In J. Spradley (ed.) *Culture and Cognition*. San Francisco: Chandler Publishing Company.

Berry, J. W. (1966) Temme and Eskimo perceptual skills, *International Journal of Psychology*, **1** (3), 207–229.

Berry, J. W. (1971) Ecological and cultural factors in spatial perceptual development, *Canadian Journal of Behavioral Science*, **3**(4), 324–336.

Berscheid, E., Dion, K., Walster, E. and Walster, G. W. (1971) Physical attractiveness and dating choice: a test of the matching hypothesis, *Journal of Experimental Social Psychology*, **7**, 173–89.

Biederman, I. (1972) Perceiving real-world scenes, *Science*, American Association for the Advancement of Science, July, Vol. 177: 77–80.

Bochner, S. (1973) The mediating man and cultural diversity, *Topics in Culture Learning*, **1**, 23–27.

Brice-Health, S. (1981) The role of ethnography in bilingual education. Lecture presented at the University of Santa Clara, Research Methods in Bilingual Education, April.

Brislin, R. W. (ed.) (1977) *Culture Learning*. Honolulu: East-West Center, University of Hawaii.

Brislin, R., Lonner, W. and Thorndike, R. (1973) *Cross Cultural Research Methods*. New York: John Wiley & Sons.

Brotherhood of St. Lawrence (1971) *Two Worlds: School and The Migrant Family*, Melbourne, Australia: Stockland Press.

Brown, R. and Lenneberg, E. H. (1954) A study of language and cognition, *Journal of Abnormal & Social Psychology*, **49**, 454–462.

Bruner, J. W. (1973) *Beyond the Information Given: Studies in the Psychology of Knowing*. J. M. Anglin (ed.), Norton.

Bruner, J. S., Oliver, R. and Greenfield, P. (1966) *Studies in Cognitive Growth*. New York: Wiley.

Burton, R. and Whiting, J. The absent father and cross-sex identity, *Merrill-Palmer Quarterly*, **7**, 85–95.

Byrne, D. (1961) Interpersonal attraction and attitude similarity, *Journal of Abnormal and Social Psychology*, **62**, 713–15.

Byrne, D. and Nelson, D. (1964) Attraction as a function of attitude similarity-dissimilarity: the effect of topic importance, *Psychonomic Science*, **1**, 93–94.

Carnoy, M. and Levin, H. (1976) *The Limits of Educational Reform*, New York: D. McKay Co.

Cazden, C. and Leggett, E. L. (1976) Culturally responsive education: a response to LAU remedies II. Paper prepared for the National Conference on Research and Policy Implications of the Task Force Report of the U.S. Office of Civil Rights. (June) Austin, Texas, quoted in Erickson *et al.*, 1978.

Cazden, C., John, V. and Hymes, D. (1972) *Functions of Language in the Classroom*. New York: Teachers College Press.

Cazden, *et al.* (1980) The contributions of ethnographic research to bicultural bilingual education, in J. Alatis (ed.), *Current Issues in Bilingual Bicultural Education*. Washington: Georgetown University Press.

Churros y Chocolate, Spanish Program, Level 1, Scott Foresman.

Cohen, E. G. (1978) *Status Equalization Project*, School of Education, Stanford University, unpublished, synopses of research report.

Cohen, E. G. (1980) Groupwork for the integrated classroom, *Stanford University Status Equalization Project*. Stanford University School of Education.

Cohen, E. G. and Roper, S. S. (1972) Modification of interracial interaction disability: an application of status characteristic theory, *American Sociological Review*, **37**, 643–657.

Cohen, E. G., *et al.* (1978) Task and authority: a sociological view of classroom management, in *Yearbook for the National Society for the Study of Education*. Illinois: University of Chicago Press, 116–43.

Coladarci, A. (1976) *Multi-Cultural Education: Some Sense and Nonsense*. Speech presented at the World Educators' Conference on Multicultural Education, Honolulu, July 13.

Cole, M. and Gay, J. (1972) Culture and memory, *American Anthropologist*, **74**(5), 1066–1084.

Cole, M. and Scribner, S. (1974) *Culture and Thought*. New York: John Wiley & Sons, Inc.

Coombs, J. (1971) *Values, Education, Rationale, Strategies and Procedures*, L. Metcalf (ed.), National Council for Social Studies, Washington.

Cziko, G., Lambert, W. E. and Gutter, R. (1979) *The impact of programs of immersion-in-a-foreign-language on pupils' social attitudes*, McGill University, unpublished draft.

Daner, F. (1974) *The American Children of Krsna*, Case studies in cultural anthropology series, G. & L. Spindler (eds.) New York: Holt, Rinehart and Winston.

Dasher (1982), J. Pusack, Iowa City, Iowa: Conduit.

Deng, F. (1972) *The Dinka of the Sudan*. Case studies in cultural anthropology series, G. & L. Spindler (eds.) New York: Holt, Rinehart and Winston.

Deregowski, J. B. (1968) Pictorial recognition in subjects from a relatively pictureless environment, *African Social Research*, **5**, 356–364(a).

Deregowski, J. B. and Serpell, R. (1971) Performance on a sorting task with various modes of representation: a cross-cultural experiment. Human Development Research Unit, University of Zambia, Report No. 18, mimeographed.

De Avila, E. (1979) Learning styles and ethnicity, speech presented to the Bilingual Education Association, Stanford University.

De Avila, E., Cohen, E. and Intili, J. (1981) *Improving Cognition: a Multi-Cultural Approach*, MICA Project, Final Report, Stanford University Center for Educational Research at Stanford.

De Avila, E. and Duncan, S. (1979) Relative linguistic proficiency and field-dependence/independence: some findings on the linguistic heterogeneity and cognitive style of bilingual children. Paper presented at TESOL Annual Convention, Boston, February.

Dolgin, J., Kemnitzer, D. and Schneider, D. (eds.) (1977) *Symbolic Anthropology*, New York: Columbia University Press.

Drills and Exercises in English Pronunciation (1971) English Language Services, New York: Collier-MacMillan.

DuBois, C. (1955) Some notions on learning intercultural understanding. In G. D. Spindler (ed.) *Education and Anthropology*, Stanford: Stanford University Press, 89–105.

Eggan, D. (1974) Instruction and affect in Hopi cultural continuity. In G. D. Spindler, *Education and Cultural Process*, New York: Holt, Rinehart and Winston, Inc.

Eisner, E. (1979) *The Educational Imagination: On the Design and Evaluation of School Programs*. New York: MacMillan.

Ekman, P. and Friesen, W. V. (1971) Constants across cultures in the fact and emotion, *Journal of Personality and Social Psychology*, **17**, 124–29.

Erikson, E. (1959) The problem of ego identity, *Psychological Issues*, **1**, 101–164.

Erikson, E. (1968) *Identity: Youth and Crisis*. New York: Norton & Co.

Erickson, F., Carrasco, R., Vera, A. and Cazden, C. (1978) *Social and Cultural Organization of Interaction in Classrooms of Bilingual Children: A Two Year Project* (July, 1978–June 1980). Working copy of the Proposal, Harvard University, School of Education.

Erickson, F. and Mohatt, J. (1977) The social organization of participation structures in two classrooms of Indian students. Paper read at AERA Conference. New York.

Festinger, L. (1957) *A Theory of Cognitive Dissonance*. Stanford, Ca.: Stanford University Press.

Fiske, S. T. (1978) How do I know thee: a review of interpersonal information processing. Unpublished manuscript, Harvard University.

Flanders, N. (1970) *Analyzing Teaching Behavior*. Reading, Mass.: Addison-Wesley Publishing Company.

Folkins, C. H., Lawson, K., Opton, E. and Lazarus, R. (1968) Desensitization and the experimental reduction of threat. *Journal of Abnormal Psychology*, **73**, 100–113.

Frake, C. O. (1962) The Ethnographic Study of Cognitive Systems, in S. Taylor (ed.) *Cognitive Anthropology*, New York: Holt, Rinehart and Winston, Inc. 1969.

Frake, C. O. (1964) in W. Goodenough (ed.) *Explorations in Cultural Anthropology*. New York: McGraw Hill, quoted in Spradley and McCurdy, 1972.

Freedman, J. L., Sears, D. O. and Carlsmith, J. M. (1981) *Social Psychology*, Englewood Cliffs: Prentice Hall, Inc.

Fuchs, L. H. (1967) The role and communication task of the change agent—experiences of the Peace Corps volunteers in the Philippines, in *Communication and Change in the Developing Countries*, D. Lerner and W. Schramm (eds.)

Gandhi, M. (1978) quoted in Preparing cross-cultural trainers, Society for Intercultural Education, Training and Research, Washington: Georgetown University Press.

Gatchel, R. and Proctor, J. (1976) Physiological correlates or learned helplessness in man, *Journal of Abnormal Psychology*, **85**, 27–34.

Geer, J., Davison, G. and Gatchel, R. (1970) Reduction of stress in humans through nonveridical perceived control of aversive stimulation, *Journal of Personality and Social Psychology*, **16**, 731–738.

Geer, J. and Maisel, E. (1972) Evaluating the effects of the pre-dictional-control confound, *Journal of Personality and Social Psychology*, **23**, 314–319.

Geertz, C. (1973) *Interpretation of Culture*. New York: Basic Books.

Glass, D. C. and Singer, J. E. (1972) *Urban Stress: Experiments on Noise and Social Stressors*. New York: Academic Press.

Glass, D. C., Singer, J., Leonard, H., Krantz, D., Cohen, S. and Cummings, H. (1973) Perceived control of aversive stimulation and the reduction of stress responses, *Journal of Personality*, **41**, 577–595.

Goodenough, W. (1964a) *Explorations in Cultural Anthropology*. New York: McGraw-Hill.

Goodenough, W. (1964b) Cultural anthropology and linguistics, in P. Garvin (ed.) *Report of the Seventh Annual Round Table Meeting on Linguistics and Language Study*, Washington: Georgetown University Series on Language and Linguistics, No. 9.

Gorden, R. L. (1970) cited in Seelye, H. N. *op. cit.*

Graham, C. (1978) *Jazz Chants*, N.Y.: Oxford University Press.

Greenberg, J. (1966) Language universals, in T. A. Sebeok (ed.) *Current Trends in Linguistics*, Vol. 3. The Hague: Mouton.

Guiora, A. Z., Brannon, R. C. L. and Dull, C. (1972) Empathy and second language learning, *Language Learning*, **22**, 111–30.

Gumpertz, J., Jupp, I. and Roberts, C. (1979) *Crosstalk: A Study of Cross-Cultural Communication*. England: National Centre for Industrial Language Training.

Hall, E. T. (1959) *The Silent Language*. Garden City, New York: Doubleday and Company, Inc.

Hamilton, D. L. and Zanna, M. P. (1972) Differential weighting favorable and unfavorable attributes in impressions of personality, *Journal of Experimental Research in Personality*, **6**, 204–12.

Hart, C. W. (1974) Contrasts between prepubertal and postpubertal education, in G. Spindler (ed.) *Education and Cultural Process*, New York: Holt, Rinehart & Winston, 342–360.

Hastorf, A. and Cantril, H. (1954) They saw a game: a case study, *Journal of Abnormal and Social Psychology*, **49**, 129–134.

Heider, E. R. (1972) Universals in color naming and memory, *Journal of Experimental Psychology*, **93**, 10–20.

Heider, F. (1958) *The Psychology of Interpersonal Relations*, New York: Wiley.

Herdt, G. (1981) *Guardians of the Flute*. New York: McGraw-Hill.

Herrell, I. C. and Herrell, J. M. (1980) Affective and cognitive aspects of bilingualism, *Nabe Journal*, **4**, 3.

Hicks, G. L. (1976) *Appalachian Valley, Case Studies in Cultural Anthropology*. New York: Holt, Rinehart & Winston.

Higgins, L. (1971) *Production of Inferences in Children*, Centre for Research in Learning and Instruction. Sydney, Australia: Government Printer.

Higgins, L. (1974) *Children's Inference Drawing: A Summarizing Report of a Psychological and Educational Study*. Centre for Research in Learning and Instruction, New South Wales Department of Education, Sydney: Government Printer.

Higgins, L. (1974) *The Production of Inferences Task*. Test and Manual, Centre for Research in Learning and Instruction. New South Wales Department of Education, Sydney: Government Printer.

Hiroto, D. S. (1974) Locus of control and learned helplessness, *Journal of Experimental Psychology*, **102**, (2), 187–93.

Hodges, B. H. (1974) Effect of valence on relative weighting in impression information, *Journal of Personality and Social Psychology*, **39**, 378–81.

Hokanson, J. E., deGood, D., Forrest, M. and Brittain, T. (1971) Availability of avoidance behavior in modulating vascularstress responses, *Journal of Personality and Social Psychology*, July 19, **1**, 60–68.

Hostetler, J. and Huntington, G. (1967) *The Hutterites in North America, Case Studies in Cultural Anthropology*, New York: Holt, Rinehart and Winston.

Hudson, W. (1962) Pictorial perception and educational adaptation in Africa, *Psychologica Africana*, **9**, 226–239.

Hudson, W. (1962) Cultural problems in pictorial perception, *South African Journal of Science*, **58**(7), 189–195.

IRI (Intercultural Relations Institute) (1982). *Take Two*. Videotape. Palo Alto, California.

Iscoe, I. and Carden, J. A. (1961) Field dependence, manifest anxiety and sociometric status in children. *Journal of Consulting Psychology*, **25**(2), 184.

Jones, E. E. and Nisbett, R. E. (1972) The actor and the observer: divergent perceptions of the causes of behavior. *Attribution: Perceiving the Causes of Behavior*. Morristown, N.J.: General Learning Press.

Kahneman, D. and Tversky, A. (1973) On the psychology of prediction, *Psychological Review*, **80**, 237–51.

Kanouse, D. E. and Hanson, L. R., Jr. (1972) Negativity in evaluations, in *Attribution: Perceiving the Causes of Behavior*, 47–62.

Kazdin, A. E. (1974) Covert modeling, imagery assessment, and assertive behavior, *Journal of Consulting and Clinical Psychology*, **43**, 716–724.

Kelley, H. H. (1972) Attribution in social interaction, in E. E. Jones, *et al.*, *Attribution Perceiving the Causes of Behavior*. Morristown, New Jersey: General Learning Press.

King, A. R. (1974) The teacher as a participant-observer: a case study, in G. Spindler (ed.) *Education and Cultural Process, op. cet.*, 399–410.

Kroeber, A. L. and Kluckhohn, C. (1952) *Culture, A Critical Review of Concepts and Definitions*. Cambridge, MA.: The Peabody Museum of American Archaeology & Ethnology, Harvard University, Vol. XLVII, No. 1.

Lambert, W. E., Gardner, R. D., Barik, H. C. and Tunstall, K. (1962) Attitudinal and cognitive aspects of intensive study of a second language, *Journal of Abnormal and Social Psychology*, **66**, 358–368.

Lambert, W. E. and Klineberg, O. (1966) *Children's Views of Foreign Peoples: A Cross-National Study*.

Lambert, W. E. and Tucker, R. G. (1972) *Bilingual Education of Children: The St. Lambert Experiment*. Rowley, Mass.: Newbury House.

Lehman, D. (1980) Personal communication.

LeVine, R. and Campbell D. (1972) *Ethnocentrism*. New York: Wiley.

Lindsay, P. and Norman, D. (1977) *Human Information Processing*, New York: Academic Press.

Lenneberg, E. H. (1967) *Biological Foundations of Language*. New York: John Wiley & Sons.

Longstreet, W. (1978) *Ethnicity: Understanding Differences in Pluralistic Classrooms*. New York: Columbia University Press.

Lozanov, G. (1978) *Suggestology and Outlines of Suggestopedy*. New York: Gordon and Breach.

Luria, A. R. (1971) Towards the problem of the historical nature of psychological processes, *International Journal of Psychology*, **6**, 259–272.

Marston, A. R. (1965) Imitation, self-reinforcement, and reinforcement of another person, *Journal of Personality and Social Psychology*, **2**, 255–261.

Marx, K. and Engels, F. (1970) *The German Ideology*. 1946. Reprint, New York: International Publishers.

McDermott, R. (1974) Achieving school failure: an anthropological approach to illiteracy and social stratification, in G. D. Spindler (ed.) *Education and Cultural Process, op. cit.*

Mead, M. (1976) Flexibility and schooling, lecture presented to the New South Wales Institute of Educational Researchers, Sydney University.

Meux, M. (1971) in *Values Education; Rationale, Strategies and Procedures*, L. Metcalf (ed.) Washington, D.C.: National Council for Social Studies.

Miller, S. (1978a) Controllability and human stress, mimeograph, Stanford University, on reserve, Main Library.

Miller, S. (1978b) Predictability and human stress, lecture presented to the Department of Psychology, Stanford University, November.

Miller, S. and Grant, R. (1978) The blunting hypothesis: a theory of predictability and human stress, in S. Bates, W. S. Dockens, K. G. Gottestan, C. Melin and S. Sjoden (eds.) *Trends in Behavior Therapy*. New York: Academic Press.

Neisser, U. (1976) *Cognition and Reality: Principles and Implications of Cognitive Psychology*. San Francisco: Freeman & Co.

Newcomb, T. M. (1961) *The Acquaintance Process*. New York: Holt.

Newcomb, T. M. (1963) Persistence and regression of changed attitudes: long-range studies, *Journal of Social Issues*, **19**, 3–14.

Nonaka, M. (1983) Correspondence regarding program evaluation meeting, Kyoto, Japan, regarding Intensive American Language and Cultural Seminar, July 1983, Center for Language & Crosscultural Skills.

Nostrand, H. L. (1966) Describing and teaching the sociocultural context of a foreign language and literature, in Albert Valdman (ed.), *Trends in Language Teaching*. New York: McGraw-Hill, pp. 1–25.

Olguin, L. (1978) Look me in the eye, educational film produced by the Santa Clara County Office of Education, as part of the series, *Cultural Clashes*, Santa Clara, California.

Osgood, C., May, W. and Miron, M. (1975) *Cross-Cultural Universals of Affective Meaning*: Chicago: University of Illinois Press.

Pelto, P. J. (1970) *Anthropological Research: The Structure of Inquiry*. New York: Harcourt, Brace.

Penfield, W. (1978) The uncommitted cortex, the child's changing brain, *Atlantic Monthly*, **214**(1), 77–81.

Pervin, L. A. (1963) The need to predict and control under conditions of threat, *Journal of Personality*, **31**, 570–587.

Philips, S. (1972) Participant structures and communicative competence: Warm Springs children in community and classroom, in Erikson *et al.*, 1978, *op. cit.*

Phillips, R. (1982) *Practicando Espanol con la Manzana II*, Iowa City, Iowa; Conduit.

Piaget, J. (1970) *Genetic Epistemology*. New York: Columbia University Press.

Politzer, R. (1978) Recent Developments in Foreign Language Education, Lecture, Stanford University, May 30.

Porter, R. and Samovar, L. (1976) Communicating interculturally, in R. Porter and L. Samovar (eds.) *Intercultural Communication: A Reader*. Belmont, CA.: Wadsworth Press.

Price-Williams, D. R. (1962) Abstract and concrete modes of classification in a primitive society, *British Journal of Educational Psychology*, **32**, 50–61.

Price-Williams, D. R. (1975) *Explorations in Cross-Cultural Psychology*. Los Angeles: Chandler & Sharp Publishers, Inc.

Price-Williams, D. R. (1980) Cognition: anthropological and psychological nexus, in G. D. Spindler, *The Making of Psychological Anthropology*. Berkeley: University of California Press.

Prosser, M. (1978) *The Cultural Dialogue*. Boston: Houghton Mifflin Company.

Ramirez, M. and Castañeda, A. (1974) *Cultural Democracy, Bicognitive Development and Education*. New York: Academic Press.

Regan, D. T. and Totten, J. (1975) Empathy and attribution: turning observers into actors, *Journal of Personality and Social Psychology*, **32**, 850–56.

Rivers, W. H. R. (1901) Introduction and vision, in A. C. Haddon (ed.) *Reports of the Cambridge Anthropological Expedition to the Torres Straits*, Vol. II, Part 1, Cambridge, England: The University Press.

Rivers, W. M. (1981) Foreword in G. L. Robinson, *Issues in Second Language and Cross-Cultural Education: The Forest Through the Trees*. Boston: Heinle & Heinle Publishers, Inc.

Robinson, C. (1978) Creating order in interethnic communication, unpublished paper, School of Education, Stanford University.

Robinson, G. L. (1978a) *Language and Multicultural Education. An Australian Perspective*. Sydney: Australian and New Zealand Book Company.

Robinson, G. L. (1978b) The magic-carpet-ride-to-another-culture syndrome: an international perspective, *Foreign Language Annals*, New York, **11**(2), 135–316.

Robinson, G. L. (1981) *Issues in Second Language and Cross-Cultural Education: The Forest Through the Trees*. Boston: Heinle & Heinle Publishers, Inc.

Robinson, G. and Slinkard, L. (1979) Differential treatment toward Chicanos: deliberate denial or reciprocal interaction? Unpublished paper, Stanford University, School of Education.

Rosenfeld, G. (1971)—*Shut those Thick Lips: A Study of Slum School Failure*, N.Y.: Hold, Rinehart and Winston.

Ross, L. (1977) The intuitive psychologist and his shortcomings: distortions in the attribution process, in L. Berkowitz (ed.) *Advances in Experimental Social Psychology*, Vol. 10, New York: Academic Press.

Saint-Exupery, A. (1946) *Le Petit Prince*, Paris: Editions Gallimard.

Sapir, E. (1973) *Selected Writings of Edward Sapir*, D. Mandelbaum (ed.), University of California Press.

Saville-Troike (1978) *A Guide to Culture in the Classroom*. Washington, D.C. Center for Applied Linguistics.

Schwartz, G. and Merton, D. (1974) Social identity and expressive symbols: the meaning of an initiation ritual, in G. Spindler (ed.) *Education and Cultural Process*, 154–175.

Seelye, H. (1973) The evolution of the stress concept, *American Scientist*, **61**, 692–99.

Seelye, H. N. (1978) *Teaching Culture: Strategies for Foreign Language Educators*, National Textbook Co. in conjunction with ACTFL.

Seligman, M. E. P. (1968) Chronic fear produced by unpredictable electric shock, *Journal of Comparative and Physiological Psychology*, **66**, 402–11.

Seligman, M. E. P. (1975) *Helplessness: On Depression, Development and Health*. San Francisco, Freeman.

Seligman, M. E. P. (1977) Reversing depression and learned helplessness, in P. Zimbardo and F. Ruch, *Psychology and Life*. Flenview, Ill.: Scott, Foresman & Company.

Shimada, M. (1983)—Correspondence regarding program evaluation of Intensive American Language and Cultural Seminar, July, 1983, Center for Language and Crosscultural Skills.

Siegel, B. (1974) Conceptual approaches to models for the analysis of the educative process in American communities, in G. Spindler, *Education and Cultural Process, op. cit.*, 39–62.

Snow, R. *et al.* (1978) *Aptitudes and Instructional Methods*: Research on individual differences in learning-related processes, under contract N00014-75, C-0882, Cybernetics Technology Office, Advanced Research Projects, Arlington, VA.

Snyder, M. and Jones, E. E. (1974) Attitude attribution when behavior is constrained, *Journal of Experimental Social Psychology*, **10**, 585–600.

Spanish Grammar (1972) C. Schmitt, N.Y.: McGraw-Hill.

Spencer, F. (1969) *Forms of Symbolic Action*, Proceedings of the 1969 annual spring meeting of the American Ethnological Society, Seattle University of Washington Press.

Spindler, G. (1974) (ed.) *Education and Cultural Process*. New York: Holt, Rinehart & Winston.

Spindler, G. (1979) *Cultural Transmission*, lectures presented winter quarter, School of Education, Stanford University.

Spindler, G. (1980) *The Making of Psychological Anthropology*. Berkeley: University of California Press.

Spindler, G. (1982) *Doing the Ethnography of Schooling: Educational Anthropology in Action*, N.Y.: Holt, Rinehart, and Winston.

Spradley, J. (1972) Foundations of cultural knowledge, in J. Spradley (ed.) *Culture and Cognition*. San Francisco: Chandler Publishing Company.

Spradley, J. and McCurdy, D. (1972) *The Cultural Experience*. Chicago: Science Research Associates.

Staub, E., Tursky, B. and Schwartz, G. (1971) Self-control and predictability: their effects on reactions to aversive stimulation, *Journal of Personality & Social Psychology*, **18**, 157–162.

Taylor, L., Catford, J., Guiora, A. and Lane, H. (1971) Psychological variables and ability to produce a second language, *Language and Speech*, **14**(2), 146–157.

Taylor, S. E. and Crocker, J. (1980) Schematic bases of social information processing, in E. T. Higgins, P. Hermann & M. P. Zanna (eds.) *The Ontario Symposium on Personality and Social Psychology*, Vol. 1 Hillsdale, N.J.: Erlbaum.

Taylor, S. E. and Fiske, S. T. (1975) Point of view and perceptions of causality, *Journal of Personality and Social Psychology*, **32**, 439–45.

Taylor, S. E., Fiske, S. T., Close, M., Anderson, C. and Ruderman, A. (1977) Solo status as a psychological variable: the power of being distinctive. Unpublished manuscript, Harvard University.

Textor, R. (1978a) Class memo, Anthropological Research Methods, ED254, Stanford University, School of Education.

Textor, R. (1978b) Class lecture on becoming a Buddhist monk, Anthropological Research Methods, ED254, Stanford University, School of Education.

Thibaut, J. W. and Riecken, H. W. (1955) Some determinants and consequences of the perception of social causality, *Journal of Personality*, **24**, 113–33.

Triandis, H. C. (1972) *The Analysis of Subjective Culture*, New York: John Wiley.

U.S. Commission on Civil Rights (1973) *Teachers and Students. Report V: Mexican American Education Study, Differences in Teacher Interaction with Mexican American and Anglo Students*. Washington, D.C.: U.S. Government Printing Office.

U.S. Department of Health, Education & Welfare, Office for Civil Rights (1975) *Task Force Findings Specifying Remedies Available for Eliminating Past Educational Practices Ruled Unlawful under Lau v. Nichols.*

Valadez, C. (1979) Cognitive benefits of bilingualism, School of Education Research Project, UCLA, private correspondence.

Warr, P. (1974) Inference magnitude, range and evaluative direction as factors affecting relative importance of cues in impression formation, *Journal of Personality and Social Psychology*, **30**, 192–97.

Weiss, J. (1971) Effects of coping behavior with and without a feedback signal on stress pathology in rats, *Journal of Comparative and Physiological Psychology*, **77**, 1–13.

Whorf, B. L. (1956) *Language, Thought, and Reality*. Boston: M.I.T. Press.

Witkin, H. A., *et al.* (1962) *Psychological Differentiation*. New York: Wiley.

Witkin, H. A. (1967) A cognitive-style approach to cross-cultural research, *International Journal of Psychology*, **2**, 233–250.

Zajonc, R. (1968) Attitudinal effects of mere exposure, *Journal of Personality and Social Psychology*, **9**(2), 1–27.

Zimbardo, P. and Ruch, R. (1977) *Psychology and Life*. Glenview, Ill., Scott, Foresman.

Index

Adler 98
Akert 51
Anglo- 57, 59, 76, 77, 98
  American 21
  Australian 55, 98
Archer 51
Aronson 63
Arunta 28, 47
Asher 31
Asian English 57
Australia 2, 3, 4, 19, 48, 66, 70

Badia 85
BAFA BAFA 95–96
Balinese 30
Bandura 89, 91, 92, 93
Bantu 22
Bartlett 54
Berlin 15
Berreman 10
Berry 19
Berscheid 65
Biederman 17, 18
British 89, 98
  English 58
Brittain 86
Brotherhood of St. Lawrence 70
Brown 15
Bruner 15, 28
Byrne 54

Cantril 63
Carlsmith 17, 49, 50, 53, 54, 62, 66
Carnoy 101
Castenada 18, 19, 21
Chicano 57, 98
Chinese 21, 51, 75
Clark 36, 37
Cohen 25, 64, 65, 78
Coladarci 99
Cole 16, 20, 23, 25
Coombs 97
Crocker 17
Cuba(n) 1
Culbertson 85

Daner 30
Dasher 35
DeGood 86
Deng 28, 29, 30, 32, 35
Deregowski 22
Dolgin 11, 101
Dinka 28, 29, 30, 32, 33, 47, 50

Eggan 34
Eisner 74
Ekman 51
Engels 13, 45
English 14, 27, 76
  English 57
Erickson 31, 47, 76
Eskimos 15

Filipino 59, 87
Fiske 68
Forrest 86
Frake 75
Freedman 17, 49, 50, 53, 54, 62, 66
French 8, 27, 75, 87
Friesen 51
Fuchs 87

Garden 19
Geertz 12, 74
Glass 88
Goodenough 10
Gorden 95
Graham 29
Grant 86
Greek 98
Guatemala 86, 90
Guiora 47
Gumperz 55, 56, 57

Hall 12
Hamilton 66
Hastorf 63
Harch 85
Hegel 11, 44
Heider 69
Herrell 28
Hicks 29
Higgins 68
Hiroto 87
Hodges 66
Hokanson 86
Holy Ghost Sect 27
Hopi 34
Hostetler 33, 35
Hudson 22
Huntington 33, 35
Hutterites 28, 30–35

India(n) 55, 56, 57, 66, 73, 98
Iscoe 19
Italian 51, 55, 63, 66, 70, 89, 93, 94

Japan(ese)   3, 4, 9, 14, 21, 24, 29, 31, 40, 42, 44–46, 51–53, 57, 63, 67, 89, 98
Jew(ish)   28, 32, 47, 83
Jones   69, 70
Jupp   55, 56, 57

Kahneman   66
Kay   15
Kazdin   91
Kelley   63
King   87
Klineberg   47
Kluckholm   13, 28
Korean   98
Kpelle   20, 25
Kroeber   13, 28
Krsna   28, 30, 34

Lambert   47, 87
Latino   76, 77
Lau versus Nichols   78
Lenneberg   15, 47
Levin   101
Lifespring   27
Lindsay   17
Lozanov   29
Luria   44

McCurdy   73, 82
McDermott   46, 78, 87
Marx   11, 13, 44, 45
Merten   33, 34
Meux   97
Mexico   30, 51, 52, 53, 75
   American   19, 21, 31, 59, 65, 75
Miller   86
Mohatt   76

Nelson   54
Newcomb   54
Nisbett   69
Nonaka   44
Norman   17
Nostrand   9

Olguin   51

Pakistan   56
Papua New Guinea   2–5, 15, 19, 22, 23, 32, 67
Peace Corps   87, 88, 89
Pelto   74
Penfield   47
Perry   41
Philips   76
Piaget   23

Polish   3, 4
Porter   11
Price-Williams   16, 17

Ramirez   18, 19, 21
Regan   70
Riecken   63
Rivers   20, 99
Roberts   55, 56, 57
Robinson   17, 27, 29, 36, 47, 50, 51, 52, 55, 63, 75, 79, 93
Roper   64, 65, 78
Rosenfeld   29, 30, 31, 78, 87
Ruch   17, 62, 85, 87

Samovar   11
San Francisco   42, 98
Sapir   10, 14
Schwartz   33, 34
Scottish   22
Scribner   16, 20, 23, 25
Sears   17, 49, 50, 53, 54, 62, 66
Seelye   79, 85, 86, 95
Seligman   85, 86, 87, 88
Serpell   22
Shimada   44
Sierra Leone   19
Singer   88
Snake Handlers   27, 90, 91
Snyder   19, 70
Spanish   2, 21, 24, 36, 54, 59, 75, 79, 80
Spencer   5, 6
Spindler   14, 76, 78, 101
Spradley   8, 73, 82
Sudan see Dinka

Take One   60
Take Two   59
Taylor   17, 68
Temne   19
Textor   74
Thibault   63
Tiv   16, 17
Totten   70
Triandis   13
Tucker   87
Turkish   50
Tversky   66

U.S. Civil Rights Commission Report (1973)   75
U.S. Department of Health, Education and Welfare (1975)   76

Vietnam(ese)   56, 59, 60, 71, 82, 83

Warr 66
Whorf 14
Witkin   18, 20

Zajonc   50, 51, 81
Zambia   22, 23
Zanna 66
Zimbardo   17, 62, 85, 87, 88